6⁰⁰

All the Green Gold

ATLANTIC OCEAN

IRELAND

LOUTH

IRISH SEA

Connemara

GALWAY

GALWAY

Galway Bay

Drogheda

River Boyne

Howth

DUBLIN

Dublin Bay

Dalkey

Killiney

River Liffey

Bray

WICKLOW

LIMERICK

Brandon Mt.

Ballyferriter

Dingle

TRALEE

Blasket

Islands

KERRY

CORK

CORK

MILES

0 10 20 30

All the Green Gold
AN IRISH BOYHOOD

Colm Luibhéid

PRAEGER PUBLISHERS

New York · Washington · London

PRAEGER PUBLISHERS
111 Fourth Avenue, New York, N.Y. 10003, U.S.A.
5, Cromwell Place, London S.W.7, England

Published in the United States of America in 1970
by Praeger Publishers, Inc.

Library of Congress Catalog Card Number: 73-123639

Printed in the United States of America

Contents

PART I: DUBLIN 1

1   *A Child and a War*   *3*
2   *Our Road*   *11*

PART II: THE BIG HOUSE
IN GALWAY

3   *The Big House*   *23*
4   *Some of the Big People*   *30*

PART III: DUBLIN 2

5   *Peadar*   *37*
6   *Granny*   *41*
7   *Night Sounds*   *45*
8   *Auntie Maggie's Farm*   *50*
9   *Sandymount National School*   *55*
10   *"Mitching" and Other Sports*   *65*
11   *Spinsters and Spinnets*   *72*
12   *Bird-Watching*   *78*

PART IV: KERRY

13 Granny and the Old Home   *85*
14 Daddy Lovett   *91*
15 Dingle   *98*
16 Things Cultural   *103*
17 Christmas and Other Holidays   *107*
18 Daddy Lovett's Last Days   *114*

PART V: SECONDARY-SCHOOL YEARS

19 Belvedere: The First Four Years   *119*
20 France   *129*
21 Belvedere: The Last Two Years   *142*

PART VI: RADIO EIREANN

22 The Routine   *151*
23 The Players   *161*

PART VII: DUBLIN 3

24 Statues, the Grand Piano, and Bang-bang   *173*
25 Christmas in Dublin   *181*
26 The Theater   *185*
27 On the Road   *188*

PART I

DUBLIN 1

I

A Child and a War

I grew up in Dublin, and, from our house near Sandymount Strand, the rumble of the bombs falling on Liverpool could be heard. Someone came to tell my father of walking along the shore during the night and seeing the leaping orange glow from the shattered city forty miles across the water from us. There was talk of the same thing happening to Dublin. I watched faces turning grim. One night, the German bombers came over Dublin to drop a deadly load on the North Strand, and, because I was a small boy and tired, I slept through all of it. In the morning, when I learned what had happened, I bitterly envied the good fortune of my elders, who had passed the black hours in fear and foreboding.

Ireland was not a participant in World War II, but echoes of that terrible holocaust kept coming into our lives in Dublin. I sat one morning in our back garden, playing with some buckets and spades—digging holes and otherwise engaged in the important tasks of a boy. Over our house came a German fighter. It could not have been more than 250 feet above ground level, and behind it was a British plane. Their guns were firing, and bits of shrapnel fell into the garden. I sat and watched, fascinated, and, as far as I was concerned, the two planes disappeared all too quickly. Sometimes the roar of anti-aircraft guns would fill the air around us. I would stand on a chair in our kitchen and look out the window, watching the shells burst in the sky above, white puffs sometimes becoming black. If the firing began while we were still out playing in the road in front of the house, helmeted figures would appear—members of the ARP, a civil-defense force composed of ordinary citizens trained for emergency duty. They came along and got us in off the streets.

From time to time, I had an opportunity to see members of this force doing things other than herding small boys to safety. One Saturday morning, I was walking along by Sandymount Strand, when, halfway down a side road, I noticed a cluster of figures, some of them familiar. They all wore helmets, and one of them had a foot pump from which a length of pipe stretched, and another had a small fire bomb. They made elaborate preparations, and eventually one of them set off the bomb. Flames shot up, and the man in charge of the pump began to work vigorously; water emerged, and somebody else held the end of the line, turned it on the fire bomb, and extinguished it. They were all so busy that they never spotted me.

Another day, my mother took my infant brother and me to a depot not far away that was also on a road off the strand. The depot was normally a resting place for trams and used to accommodate as many as a dozen of them at a time, and it was always a thrill for me to be taken there to look at them. On this particular day we came with a different purpose. We took our place in a line of people. Eventually, we reached a table where a benign lady with white hair took our names and then produced two gas masks from a big cardboard box beside her. She could give us only two: There were no masks for babies. We tried them on and brought them home but, fortunately, never had to use them. Mine was kept in a box in my room. The few times I did put it on, I began to perspire immediately and the eyepiece fogged up so that I could not see anything.

My father got his mask some days before we did. He came home from the school where he taught, and casually walked into the house wearing it. For an instant, I did not recognize him, and the apparition in our house terrified me. My father made himself known as quickly as he could, but, for a while, I was beyond consolation.

When I was six, I began to read about the war. Each morning my father began his day by reading the *Irish Press*, and I sat beside him and looked over his shoulder at diagrams showing the position of armies and at pictures of the latest events. I regularly acquired—I do not remember how—copies of *The War Illustrated*, a magazine filled with pictures of Spitfires and Hurricanes in action, of British generals and airmen, of aircraft carriers and transports, of planes of the Fleet Air Arm. And we listened to the radio, to the broadcasts from London, particularly the voice of Frank Phillips, one of the most famous of the BBC announcers, who read the news in precise, dispassionate tones, every syllable clearly given its due weight. And the news rolled on. One afternoon, while I was playing on the road outside my house, an English jeweler emerged from his doorway across on the other side, came down to his gate, and called over to me, "General Alexander has entered Rome." Then he put his hands in his pockets and smiled up and down.

I sat one morning with my father as he looked at the front page of the *Irish Press*. In one corner was a picture of Hitler, and beside it was a single column describing how a plot to kill him had failed. It was the plot of July 20, 1944.

Then would come a reminder of what was happening elsewhere. The sirens would sound, and people would wonder. One morning, a little after nine o'clock, when my father had gone to work, the sirens howled and it was clear that this was a full-scale alarm. My mother picked my brother out of his cot, and she and my Aunt Niamh went down the hall in our house, through a doorway, and in under the granite steps that mount on either side of the front of the house. From the hall, my mother fetched a black carved wooden chair with a high, straight back and carried it into the small, lightless room under the stairs where the gas and electric meters were kept. My aunt sat on the chair and held my brother. I stood beside her, and my mother was near the door. We listened. There was the distant sound of aircraft and then silence. After a while my mother ventured out to the front door, opened it cautiously, and looked out. We were all very quiet, and, shortly afterward, the all-clear sounded.

The older people talked about air-raid shelters, evacuation, contingency planning. Inevitably, the stories began to spread of strange happenings in the city, of German parachutists seen, of submarines landing in the west of Ireland. There were people who swore that they knew a man who knew a man who had been in a remote pub in the west of Ireland where a German submarine crew and an English one had come in for refreshments, and that for a moment there was a truce. But, when they had all downed their Guinnesses or their whiskeys or whatever they were consuming, the crews went their separate ways out into the Atlantic to continue their grim work.

One story that has always lingered in my memory concerned the building of an air-raid shelter in midtown, near the river. I was told that a massive wall had to be built on one side of the shelter and that, while the work was in progress, the laborers unwittingly enclosed an entire printing plant inside. It was only sometime after the completion of the shelter that someone became aware of the fact that the printing plant had vanished. And the story was embellished, as such stories always are in Dublin. I heard one man claim not only that the presses had been enclosed in the wall but also that the typographers who were busily going about their business at the time had been encased in the shelter. For years, I carried in my mind a picture of a group of typographers frozen before their keys, encased within their concrete surroundings, patiently waiting for the end of the war and doomed to wait forever because, when the hostilities were over, a civil servant had forgotten where the printing plant had stood.

There were tales of spies who had landed in unlikely places. There were stories of enemy agents who had landed on remote hillsides or dropped into the middle of bogs and who had been rescued by the local inhabitants and thawed out with generous dosages of whiskey or whatnot. Our belief in the truth of these tales was supported when we would read in the papers from time to time about Germans who had dropped into Ireland and been picked up. After the war, we saw pictures of one of them. He had been incarcerated in Mountjoy Gaol in Dublin, and we saw him with his new bride. He was granted a week's honeymoon, and the photographers were there to take pictures of him

as he left the jail with his smiling wife, to move off for a
week of peace and privacy somewhere in Ireland before
he would have to return to his cell.

There was rationing, too, and this created many problems. Supplies were sometimes quite short, and there were
times when my infant brother proved very useful. He was
entitled to a child's ration, but he had not yet reached the
age when he was either willing or able to consume it. So
we got his allowance of tea and sugar and butter to supplement the allowance that was available for the rest of us in
the house. Bread, if kept overnight, turned green and
moldy. There was a great shortage of fruit, other than what
could be grown at home. One night, a government minister
went on the radio to tell the housewives of Ireland of a
device known as the "straw box." Because supplies of coal
were very limited, there was very little gas for cooking.
But, if a piece of meat was brought to a boil the night
before it was required, and if it was then put in its warm
container into a box packed with straw, a fully cooked
joint would emerge the next morning. Scientific friends
have told me since that this is a perfectly normal, compre-
hensible process, but to me it seemed an astonishing one,
and it still does.

With the shortage of gas, there appeared the great
boogeyman of Dublin, the "glimmer man." When the local
gas supply had been cut off for the day, after two or two
and a half hours, there was sometimes a residue that was not
powerful but that sufficed for boiling a kettle of water or
doing some short-order cooking. It was illegal to make use
of this "glimmer," as it was called, and inspectors of the
Dublin Gas Company were sent around to various houses,
arriving unexpectedly and having the right to demand admission. If a householder was found to have a warm gas
stove during the off hours, he was liable to prosecution.

So the glimmer man was one of the dreaded figures of the city, because sometimes the supply of gas was so low that only by using the glimmer as well as the legal amount was it possible for families to get by.

Over all of this presided a mysterious, remote figure whom those I listened to called, simply, "Dev." They talked of Dev standing up to Churchill and keeping the country safe, and of the need to tell Dev this or that. After a while I began to connect this strange figure with the photographs I saw in my father's paper, pictures of a bespectacled man who was described as Mr. de Valera. At one point, when the effects of rationing were most keenly felt, a song made the rounds. The only part that remains in my memory includes the following nicely ambiguous lines:

> Bless them all, bless them all, bless them all,
> The long and the short and the tall!
> God bless de Valera and Sean McEntee!
> Bless the black bread and the half ounce of tea.

Then the war was over, and, for the first time since I was two or three years old, I saw oranges and bananas. A man of whom I knew, who made a fortune smuggling bags of sugar into England (sacks with the real thing on top and filled underneath with sand), switched to other, equally profitable, enterprises. The smuggling of tea from the north of Ireland eased off. There was an end to the tales of smuggling that people exchanged around me, such as the one about a woman who was bringing a packet of tea across the border in her knickers and, when the excitement of passing through customs was over, exclaimed, "Oh, dear, girls, I'm afraid I've wet the tea!" Or there was the story of a London housewife who received a turkey from her brother in Ireland. It was sewn shut at the appropriate places, and so she assumed it contained the usual Christmas stuffing. It was only later, upon hearing an explosion from inside the oven, that she discovered that it had, indeed, been stuffed, but with a bottle of whiskey.

Rationing, too, came to an end. Englishmen and their families came in off the boat to sample genuine meat and to try to forget the long years of privation. Over Dublin Bay, on an occasional Saturday, American planes would fly from Germany. They would land at the airport, and the crew would start in toward the city to the Dolphin Restaurant, where steaks were awaiting them. Then they headed back to the airport again and took off. I wondered how they accounted for the mileage of these trips in their log books.

But, most of all, I noticed in the faces of my parents and their friends that they seemed able to relax. A burden had been lifted from their shoulders, and, naturally, I was glad.

2

Our Road

At the top of the road where we lived in Dublin was
an old martello tower that overlooked the strand, and
Sandymount Strand, in turn, spread out to become the
enfolding arms of Dublin Bay, with the Hill of Howth on
one side and Dunlaoighre on the other. At the opposite
end of the road was a church, a structure of the nineteenth
century, with gargoyles and a lawn around it. And facing
this was a big red house at least three stories high, surrounded by trees and with an ample garden at the back.
In this house lived the minister who took charge of the
Church of Ireland parish in the neighborhood. When I was
a small boy, the incumbent was a thin, elderly man who

wore spectacles. He was married, quiet, and a scholar. We heard, from time to time, that he was in trouble with his superiors for allowing such outrageous practices as having crosses in his church, and other paraphernalia smacking too strongly of Catholicism.

He was not the only ecclesiastic on our road. Opposite our house was an Anglican convent, and it, too, had its minister, who came to live in the first house of the row in front of us. For many years, throughout my boyhood and teens, the minister there was an Englishman. Red-faced and extremely genial, he had a habit of clearing his throat so loudly that he could be heard from one end of the road to the other. It was a long, slow, booming gurgle, which rose to a note of satisfaction and echoed up and down the street. He had a blackthorn stick, and he spoke to everybody. Indeed, he was so popular that, among the small boys on the road, the question arose early as to why he should not be called Father. He did, after all, wear a collar and stock; he wore black; and there was no doubt about the fact that he conducted the services for the nuns in his convent. The question of whether the minister should be called Father agitated us considerably. For a while, because we liked him, we decided we would address him in this way, and we did so for a number of weeks. Then, somewhere, an unecumenical note was introduced, and, for some reason that I have completely forgotten, we reverted to calling him Mister. We did so loudly and ostentatiously, so as to make it clear to him that a matter of Catholic action was involved. There is no doubt that, if he did notice our changed attitude, he was merely amused, for that was the kind of man he was.

He laughed a good deal, and his laugh, like the clearing of his throat, could be heard from one end of the road to the other. He had a wife and family, too, and, every so often, we saw the members of his family arriving from England. For a Dublin boy, the fact that the minister had a wife was quite ordinary. It was not until I had gone to Kerry and similar places that it was brought home to me that there was anything very astonishing about a married clergyman, and I can recall the amazement of a cousin when I mentioned the fact that the two ministers who lived near us were married, adding that farther down the road was a man who was cousin to a bishop, and the bishop also had a wife. It was then I heard the saying, filled with the ambiguity in which Kerrymen excel, having to do with the difference between a priest and a minister: *"Bionn bean ag an ministeir, ach bionn cailin ag an sagart."* ("The minister has a woman, but the priest has a girl.")

The convent facing our house was inhabited by a small community of nuns whom we rarely saw. They appeared only minutes before the local bus was due to leave for midtown. But their presence was brought home to us especially during the night. They had a chapel, and, at two and six o'clock every morning, the chapel bell would ring. Many a night, as I lay snug and warm in my bed, I pitied the nuns who had to get out of the warmth of their own beds and go down and pray, or do whatever they did in their chapel in the back of the convent. But, except for the tolling of their bell, they entered little into the lives of their neighbors.

Halfway up the road was a bachelor in his fifties. He lived with his mother, and he took off for work every morning at eight-thirty. He used to come home early in the afternoon, and I often met him on the bus, where he invariably talked to me about Shakespeare, of whom he was passionately fond. He would sometimes declaim while he sat there with his cigarette. Frequently, it was the funeral speech of Mark Antony. And sometimes he would declaim

so loudly and with such insistence that other passengers
would turn to look at him. But it was not until many years
later that I came to realize that there was a direct relation
between the loudness of his recitation and the amount of
Guinness he had consumed during the day. But he was a
nice man, and he was generous. Frequently, he would slip
me sixpence or a shilling to go off and buy myself some
chocolate or a magazine.

At the head of the road lived a little lady, Maggie, who
spent many years as principal teacher in one of the rough-
est, toughest kindergartens in the center of Dublin. Barely
five feet tall, she was almost completely blind and had a
marked Dublin accent, and she was one of the most popular
and benevolent little figures that I have ever encountered.
When I first came to know her, she had a marvelous car,
a Morris built in the 1930's. It was very solid. It was put
away during the war, and, one day, after seven years, she
poured some gas into it and turned the key, and the car
started off again, proving entirely reliable and faithful until
the time came for her to quit driving, which she finally
did when she could no longer distinguish between persons
on the road and shadows cast by the street lamps. I traveled
in that car often. It was roomy inside and had a very large
luggage compartment at the back, as well as numerous
devices that I did not understand then, nor do I today.
But one of the most spectacular aspects of the car was its
system of jacks. A button, when pushed, would cause four
jacks to drop down simultaneously under the car, to raise
it off the ground. On more than one occasion, Maggie
found herself quite puzzled by the fact that, even though
she had put her car in gear and had let out the clutch,
nothing seemed to happen. There was the sound of the
engine revving up and nothing more. Somebody would
point out that the car was up on jacks again, and she would

take it out of gear and press the appropriate button, and the car would drop back down onto its wheels.

Because she was so small, Maggie had to have three cushions at her back. During one period, when there was a prolonged bus strike in Dublin, I used to ride with her every day, sitting behind her. One morning I realized that she could scarcely see beyond the front of the car. At one point along the road into the city, there used to be a bridge consisting of three semicircular iron frames. The middle frame served to divide the road. I often used to notice, as we approached the crossing, sometimes at forty miles an hour, that Maggie would straighten up and give the cushions an extra little tug, and her eyes would get narrower and narrower until, finally, they were barely slits, and I always used to wonder if she would make it over the bridge, but somehow she always did.

She had many misadventures in that car. Frequently, as we drove through Dublin or stopped at a traffic light, she would point to a large plate-glass window in a shop and say, "I drove through that once." On O'Connell Street, some repair work was going on one time, resulting in an enormous hole in the center of the roadway, surrounded, of course, by protective barriers. She drove right through the barriers and into the hole and had to be lifted out by a crane. On another occasion, also on O'Connell Street, she was at the head of a line of cars waiting to cross an intersection. She became distracted and failed to see the officer on duty signaling her to move. Eventually, he walked slowly over and stuck his head in the window. "D'you want me to lead you across by the lily-white hand?" he asked. And Maggie, who always had a fear of men, cringed in the seat, letting her foot off the clutch, and the car lurched forward, almost beheading the guard. Another unfortunate policeman, who came to offer help one evening when her car had stalled, arrived just in time to have his foot run over as the car started off.

We had another neighbor—a man called Aloysius, who had no family and whose wife seemed to have little use for him. He meant well, but his life was a constant series of sadly unachieved plans. Once, when his wife went to visit her sisters in England, Aloysius decided to surprise her by having a completely new kitchen installed. It included a range. When everything was complete, Aloysius started the range working the day before his wife was due to return, and something went wrong. Nobody is quite sure exactly what it was. All that is clear is that Aloysius appeared suddenly, panic-stricken, with a bucket of water. He climbed to the roof of his house and poured the bucket of water down the chimney. There was a dull explosion inside, and, when he went back into the house, the kitchen and the adjacent living room were a complete shambles.

Aloysius worked for the Department of Agriculture, and, from time to time, the papers would report an outbreak of foot-and-mouth disease somewhere in England. Aloysius would hurry off on his bicycle, and we always got the impression from what he told us that he had gone to seal off Ireland by closing its ports and ending the flow of all traffic into and out of the country. As small boys we were quite awed that one man should have such power.

At the top of the road, where the tower was, there was a store where my mother used to go to get her groceries. Outside this store on summer Sundays, a group of women and men would gather around a portable organ, which one of them would play while the others sang hymns. When they had finished, one of them would produce an old wooden box that had once contained dried fish. Someone would stand on the box and give a sermon to all the others who were gathered in the circle. They all would look very solemn and attentive. Then, somebody else would get up, and the routine would be repeated. As far as I could make out, it was always the same group that took part in the ceremonies, which seemed never to vary. Why they took the trouble to come there was something I could not quite understand, but it was one of the excitements of a fine Sunday afternoon to go out and sit on the wall overlooking the beach and listen to the hymns and wonder what all the talk was about.

It was, perhaps, the entertainment afforded by these people that led me, from then on, to feel a certain admiration for all kinds of hot gospelers. In later years, when I used to go to school in the center of Dublin, there was one group that came every Friday night to the corner of a certain side street. Six little old women would sit in a circle and sing hymns. They sang any hymns we requested, and one we particularly enjoyed was called, "When I Get to Heaven." We would ask them regularly to sing this for us, and we would stand back while the six ladies and a rather deficient squeeze-box would perform this or some other offering. In addition to the singers, there were usually two speakers, one of them a lady dressed completely in black, who was reputed to be the niece of Charles Stuart Parnell, the great Irish parliamentarian and orator. If she was, she certainly inherited his talents for speaking over hecklers, because we heckled her unmercifully, and she ignored us completely and spoke with much effect. Her companion was a man who had spent years as a missionary teaching in Rhodesia. He was a gentle, courtly man who treated every ill-mannered question and interruption by schoolboys such as myself with extreme deference and patience. They gathered there every Friday night for years, and, the last time I saw him, he told me he had decided to learn Irish and to go off to some of the rural areas of Ireland to preach. I often wondered afterward what became of him, because I can well imagine that, if he had arrived in some remote area in the west or southwest, he would certainly have been greeted with immense curiosity.

In the summers, too, the crowds would come from the city out to Sandymount to spend the day on the beach. It was then that I began to get to know the differences in accents that prevailed within Dublin. There were those who came from Drimnagh; there were those who came from Crumlin. Some came from midtown and some from a little beyond. They all had their own accents, and they provided me with endless insights into the varied life of the city in which I was living. All sorts of characters would come, too. I used to follow with the greatest interest a man we called Gandhi. Why he was called Gandhi I am not sure, but I suspect it was because he was bald, which does not seem a very good reason. Gandhi used to know all the children in the neighborhood. After coming down our road, he would shuffle toward the beach, and we would see him heading off toward an old wrecked bath, which was used long ago but of which only the shell remained. And then word went out that Gandhi was inside. What was particularly exciting about that bit of news was the inference that Gandhi was standing there with all those cockleshells drifting in through the one hole that went into the old baths, and that he was doing calisthenics. He raised his hands and lowered them. He tried to touch his toes. He tried to touch his knees. He bent backward and forward. He did jerks. Many a time I joined the line of small boys on the top of the bath wall, and we peeked over and watched Gandhi as he stood inside there, walking up and down and performing those various astonishing gyrations.

As I came back down the road from the beach, I passed a house where two sisters lived, teachers, who were very pious. We used to see them hurrying to Mass every Sunday morning, or to Benediction in the afternoon, or, during Lent, going off to Rosary in the church every day after tea. They were a remarkable pair. The older of the two completely dominated her younger sister, to the extent that, whenever they walked out—the older sister in front, the younger behind—and encountered anybody, they reacted in perfect unison, like two members of a well-trained chorus. The older sister would smile and say to me, "Aren't you a good boy?" and the younger would echo, ". . . good boy?" Or the older would say, "We must hurry off now," and the younger would echo, ". . . hurry off now." When they smiled, the older sister would cock her head to one side, and the younger did precisely the same. The timing was quite remarkable. It must have taken years to achieve it.

In another house was a bank clerk, who lived with his elderly mother and sister. Every morning he got up early, and over the road would echo the strains of Bach. The bank clerk sat at the piano and played until five minutes before it was time for him to run off to work. Sometimes, he sang to his own accompaniment, and his singing was awful, but his playing was perfect. Every morning he did this, and he would return at the end of the day, have a quick meal, and rush in to the piano, which he would proceed to play for hours. At night, he would not bother to draw the blinds in the living room, and we could see him there at the piano, rocking back and forth as he played and played and played. He was one of the few men I have seen who counted the minutes until retirement, and, when he finally did give up his work, he was able to do what he had wanted to do all his life. From morning to night, he sat at his piano, and he continued to sing in that off-key voice of his. He seemed totally happy.

I passed by his house and turned into our own, which

was built at the turn of the century. Peadar, my grandfather, had bought it and made it into two self-contained apartments, the lower apartment being then, as now, occupied by my parents. Until 1943, various tenants used to live upstairs. When I was a child, the upper apartment was occupied by a German diplomat, a charming man who was very popular among the bachelors in the neighborhood. His manner was impeccable, but his English was not, so that, on one occasion, when he had been delayed by traffic and had reached a dinner party late, the apology he offered his hostess was, "I got constipated in the traffic." His career in Dublin was marked by many such famous lapses of language, but, for all that, he was widely esteemed. Around the outbreak of World War II, he was transferred from Ireland to South America, and his successor upstairs was a lawyer who installed a wife and a white dog. Their coming was marked for the most part by noise and thumps. I did not see them very often, but their presence upstairs was always evident. Day in, day out, there were shouts and bangs and an occasional shriek; invited guests seemed prone to falling on the floor or over the furniture. But they did not stay long, for, early in 1943, my grandfather sold his house in Galway, moved to Dublin, and came to live in the apartment upstairs.

PART II

THE BIG HOUSE IN GALWAY

3

The Big House

The coming of my grandfather meant the end of my trips to Galway, where I had spent my first holidays as a child. We used to take the train from Westland Row in Dublin, and, because of the war, there was no certainty as to how long it would take to reach our destination. The train was rarely on time, and I have a faint memory of relatives' trying to keep me amused during the journey. When we arrived, we would travel on one of the few taxis operating in the city; it took us to Salthill, from which there was a view of Galway Bay, the Clare hills, and the Atlantic beyond.

At Salthill the car would turn right into a road called

Rockbarton, a tree-lined road with one big red house on the left. We drove past it until we reached two silver gates that were always open to the long driveway leading up to the home of my mother's family. As we turned in, I could see the words "St. Mary's" on the gateposts. There was the glimpse of a field on our left, and on the right a tennis court, around which clusters of daffodils would grow in the spring. The car turned past bushes of fuschia and came to a halt in front of a high door, where my grandparents—Granny and Peadar, as I called them—were waiting with other members of the family to bid us welcome.

Granny was small, very thin, and white-haired. Peadar was taller and had a thick ginger moustache, which he would stroke regularly at mealtimes. Once inside the door, we were in a large hall. There was a winding staircase, there were pictures around the walls, and at one side was a black grandfather clock, which fascinated me. Every night, Peadar would take the head off it. He would produce a key, and, as he wound, there would be a long grating noise and the two heavy weights would rise to the top. He would put the head back, and then, through the rest of that night and the following day, the solid, massive ticking of the clock would echo through the house.

Beyond the hall was a corridor, and off the corridor on either side were many rooms. I have forgotten how many, but I have a distinct recollection of a large drawing room with heavy furniture, most of it acquired at auctions in Ireland or England or on the Continent. The carpets were thick. There was an ornate sofa, and beautifully framed paintings hung on the walls. There was a piano with two movable candle-holders, which reached out and presumably, in some earlier day, had provided the light by which a recital was carried on. There was a heavy marble mantelpiece and, on it, a green marble clock with gold pillars. It was a well-lighted room, for the windows were enormous and looked out over a lawn and a garden.

Nearby was a dining room, and my main recollection is of a twelve-foot-long table, which could be extended by the addition of leaves. The floor was carpeted, and there were mahogany sideboards in which silverware was kept. All around the room were pieces of silver, bowls, kettles that were not used, a tea set on a tray. There were silver candlesticks, silver knives and forks with cut-glass handles, and cut-glass bowls with silver rims. In one corner was a large press for storing dinnerware and glasses. The light that shone over the expanse of the table came from another of those vast windows on the bottom floor, a window that also looked out on the lawn and garden, on the far wall and the blue sky.

Where the corridor ended, one pushed through into the kitchen and its associated network of smaller rooms. Beyond were a dairy and a yard full of storehouses.

I went up the carpeted spiral staircase to my bedroom, in which there were a double bed against the wall, a crib, a wardrobe, a dressing table, a chest of drawers, and a washstand. The floor was carpeted; the walls, papered; the ceiling, painted white. In the room, light was provided by a French window, which one could step through onto a balcony surrounded by a highly ornate wrought-iron railing painted silver.

In this house and in the fields around it, I learned to play and to find my own amusements, to join in the fun of companions who came to visit me from houses in the neighborhood. I spent a great deal of time in the kitchen, where I enjoyed watching Granny at work. And she was helped by a maid called Annie, a girl who had come to "St. Mary's" from an Irish-speaking area of poor farms and poor land in Connemara. She wore a black dress and a white pinafore. Although she was young, she had a lined face, but the lines were mostly around her eyes and came, I believe, from the fact that she was almost always cheerfully laughing. I tormented her unmercifully, and she was too kind to retaliate in any effective way.

It was a very large kitchen—one whole wall was taken up by an enormous black range, into which baskets of turf were regularly poured and on which the cooking was done. There was a long wooden table at one corner; the hired hands used to come to this table from their work in the fields. Annie would serve them, heaping their plates with meat and vegetables and potatoes out of the big pots on the stove.

One of these men with whom I had become quite friendly was called Arthur. I admired him immensely, for all sorts of accomplishments: for the way he worked in the fields, for the way he sprayed the potatoes, but most of all for the way he ate. Arthur would come in at one o'clock every day to have his dinner, and on his plate Annie would put some meat, some vegetables, and half a dozen large potatoes. What always astonished me, and the reason I was always lurking in the kitchen at this hour, was the fact that Arthur could take these potatoes, divide them into quarters, and then proceed to swallow each quarter whole. In doing so, his jaw would rise slightly, as if to make room somehow. I admired him enormously for this and tried to imitate it myself when I ate with my grandparents in the big dining room, but the results were never so satisfactory.

Off the kitchen were a number of smaller rooms. There was a dairy in the middle of which stood an enormous butter churn. Underneath a window, there was a shelf bearing pans of buttermilk, which, to my continual mystification, visitors seemed to want to drink.

The back yard opened out on a series of small storehouses, and, from this yard, one moved on into fields that seemed very extensive to me. There was one field close by that Peadar used for pasture. Beyond that was another in which he grew row after row of potatoes and other vegetables. As a small boy I used to go out to watch him or the hired hands, particularly at spraying time, envying them as they walked up and down the rows, each man with a tank on his back. Each tank had a handle to be gripped by the right hand, and, as it was worked up and down, a thin stream of greenish yellow liquid came out of a nozzle held in the left hand. It was supposed to be good for the crops.

There was much to explore—bushes, trees, the back garden with an orchard. There were the beehives and a greenhouse where Peadar grew grapes. I had not seen grapes growing before, and I spent many hours in the greenhouse, examining the vines and wondering about this curious fruit I had never seen in Dublin. There were chickens somewhere around in back, and I remember sneaking into the henhouse and stealing about a dozen eggs. Then, disappearing into a corner behind some trees, I set up a mound of stones and hurled the eggs one at a time at it until a dirty yellow mass had accumulated, and I went off then quite satisfied.

In Granny's house I used to get involved in Ruaidhri's amusements. He was an uncle, only five or six years older than myself, with whom I fought for every possible reason. I remember watching him with considerable envy as he cycled up the side of a mound on the field in front of the house. In the back wheel of the bicycle he had put a stiff piece of cardboard, so that, when he got up speed, it sounded as if he were driving a motorcycle, and I envied him greatly for the fact that he could ride a bicycle and that I was just a bystander.

Another day, Ruaidhri got a thick ball of string; he took two tin cans, cut the bottom out of each, and replaced the bottoms with paper. He put a hole in each piece of paper, slipped in the string, and made a knot, so that the string would hold. Then, he set this up in a tree at one end of the field opposite the house and extended the string diagonally all the way to the other end of the field, where there were more trees. There, he set up the other can. Apparently, the idea was that, if you spoke into the can on either end, a message would come through to the other end as on radio. I remember insisting that I be included in this, and Ruaidhri, because he was a patient uncle, although I am sure he must have found me a repulsive nephew, cut off a length of string, unearthed a third can, and attached it to his line so that I could join in the activity. I don't think I heard any message loud and clear, but at least I had the satisfaction of being involved. It was good fun and passed an entire sunny afternoon pleasantly.

On another occasion, and as a great treat, I was given permission to go with Ruaidhri and his friend to spend the night in a tent that had been set up in a field opposite the house. Between this field and the house was a road, and, beyond the road, fields stretching away to Salthill and the sea. We went out, shouted and played, jumped around and chatted. The night got darker. Finally, when we opened the flap and looked out, we could see the stars. We had a small light, and we rolled ourselves up in blankets. A moment came when we suddenly grew very silent and chilled as steps sounded out on the road. Somebody came walking by, and we dared not even whisper. In our imagination, it was somebody who would come and surely strike us if he knew of our presence. I suspect now it was either my father or Peadar, coming to see what we were doing, for I gathered that, throughout the night, those in the house got very little sleep because of the continual shouts and laughter and other sounds of enjoyment that came from our field.

4

Some of the Big People

In the 1930's, I was too young to pay much attention to what the adults did in the big house. But I did know that open house was held every Sunday. From all parts of Galway and farther away, many people gathered for sessions that were mostly dominated by talk in Irish. There was music, there was singing, there was recitation, and there was discussion. Granny and each of her children were musical and could play some instrument. And so they had their own little chamber orchestra and could perform, and they did so on many occasions. Men who were devoted to the revival of the Irish language, of old Irish music and songs, came too, and they sang and played and talked about these. There were some who came to talk and some who came to play cards, and there was much gaiety in the house at these times.

Some of the people who came to these sessions were unusual. One, for example, was an Englishman who had come over to Ireland in 1919 and concluded, upon arrival, that Ireland had suffered grievously over too many long years from English occupation. As a mark of protest, he had decided never to speak English again and to settle in Ireland. He came from a very well-known English family: One of his cousins had become a bishop; another, an admiral; and both had been well known and highly decorated during World War I. This man, as part of his transformation, had turned to wearing kilts. He traveled around various parts of the country, urging on the nationalist movement and, in particular, the movement to revive the use of the Irish language. He had bought a large house some miles outside of Galway, and he continues, to this day—he is a very old man now—to wear kilts and to speak Irish. As a great concession to non-Irish-speakers, he will converse in French. He is quite well known, and he will accept nothing English. Even in the buses and the shops, where the money can be a mixture of English and Irish, he refuses to accept English coins as change, and most people try to oblige him.

Another regular visitor to the house was a colleague of Peadar's in the civil service. He had married rather late in life, but he was determined to raise his children to speak only Irish. When he had once caught his two boys speaking English, he had locked them in their room with instructions to write an essay in Irish on "Why I Spoke English."

These open houses on Sundays meant the arrival of very many people, and, for Granny's children—that is, my mother and her brothers and sisters—these occasions meant dressing up, being on their best behavior, being polite, and performing and singing for the assembled guests. There was croquet on the lawn outside when the weather was good, and those who did not want to sing or play or discuss could sit on the deck chairs with a view of the garden, which was walled off and had covered walks with wooden archways and roses and other flowers of every description. There were garden seats as well. There were costumes of various kinds, from the sober Sunday best of Peadar to the gaily colored kilts of some of the visiting men.

Peadar would wear a suit with a waistcoat, and in the waistcoat pocket was a big gold watch with a gold chain that stretched across his stomach. He rolled his own cigarettes. Out of one of his waistcoat pockets, he drew small sheets of paper; from another, he pulled a little device that I greatly admired and would occasionally try to use when nobody was looking. What I admired most about Peadar in this matter was that, besides being able to roll cigarettes with this strange gadget, he could, if need be, do so on his bicycle, with one hand. This to me was a marvelous feat. When the cigarettes were rolled and ready, they invariably had a few wisps of tobacco dripping from them, and Peadar would light his cigarette and begin to smoke. Even as a child, I sometimes wondered if his moustache was in danger of catching fire. But, of course, I need not have worried.

Peadar was in charge of the local customs house. This was a rather gloomy red brick building with a whole series of dim offices. He worked in a room that had no windows at all. He had many responsibilities, one of which was keeping track of all the bonded whiskey in the west of Ireland. He sat behind a desk and wrote the details of shipments, warehouses, and bonds into large, solidly covered ledgers. Sometimes, he would have to go on trips through neighboring districts, inspecting various customs posts. On the rare occasion when a transatlantic airplane landed in Galway (in the 1930's, such landings were not too numerous), Peadar, as chief customs officer in the region, would have to go out and inspect the plane. The airport is in a place called Oranmore, about five miles from the city. It was then, and is now, no more than a field, which dips alarmingly, so that a hump rises in the center, and the grass is cropped by sheep. Presumably then, as now, incoming pilots had to allow not only for the condition of the landing field but also for the fact that a stray sheep or, indeed, a whole flock might get in his way. After the planes landed, Peadar would inspect their passengers' luggage. Some transatlantic liners called at the Galway harbor, and Peadar would have to go down and see that his men were properly stationed and going about their business.

Once, when a liner had landed its passengers, Peadar noticed a girl coming ashore laden with heavy luggage. He took pity on her; it was obvious to his well-practiced eye that she could hardly be smuggling in anything of consequence. It was also obvious to him that she would be greatly wearied by having to stand in line and wait for clearance. So he went up to her and offered to take her luggage out. He picked up her bags and carried them through, and the other customs officers naturally made way. When they got outside, she expressed her gratitude, pulled out her purse, and, after hunting carefully, produced a shilling, which she offered him as a tip. Because he was Peadar, he thanked her warmly, went away, and, for years afterward, derived great pleasure from telling the story of how he was mistaken for a porter.

Much of his responsibility concerned the distribution of liquor in the west of Ireland. Bonding and so forth took many hours of his time. Illegal liquor was also a problem. There was then in the west of Ireland, as there is now, a flourishing industry that produced illegal poteen, a colorless liquor distilled from barley; when it is colorless, it is reasonably safe and is guaranteed, if rubbed on the joints, to help relieve rheumatism. If taken internally, it is guaranteed to warm the recipient. If it is not colorless, however, it can be very dangerous and cause serious physical and mental breakdown. Peadar, as chief customs officer of the west, was naturally responsible for trying to stamp out this illegal distilling. Of course, it was a hopeless task, but, being a conscientious man, he went about it as best he could. One of the associated problems was to try to stop the distribution of this illegal liquor, and it was not until many years after he had retired that he finally learned where, during his years with customs and excise, a central cache of poteen was to be found in Galway. It had been set up in his own barn, on his own farm. What safer place for the distillers to keep their wares than on the property of the man who was chiefly responsible for trying to stamp out the operation?

PART III

DUBLIN 2

5

Peadar

When Granny and Peadar left Galway early in 1943, they came to live in the apartment over ours. For them, the move was a return to familiar places, because they had lived in Dublin before and had owned a house that overlooked Sandymount Strand.

Peadar adjusted well to the prospect of retirement, and he could look back on a long career. He had come of a family in County Louth, and, like many of his brothers and sisters, he had been compelled to leave the farm to seek a living elsewhere. He joined the old British Customs and Excise Service, and his duties brought him for periods of varying duration to Wales, England, Scotland, and many parts of Ireland. While he was in London, he learned Irish, a language that he mastered and spoke for the rest of his life. He made many friends, and then he got married. He and Granny lived awhile in Wales, and Granny used to tell me of waking up in the early hours of black winter mornings and hearing the miners marching through the gloom and the cold to work, filling the dark with their songs. Later came the transfer to Dublin, and, soon after, he was sent to Galway.

Now, in 1943, he was back again, and he became a part of my boyhood years. The images of him crowd in, and the need to choose among them seems a little unfair, as it must always seem in the case of a person one loves. I listened as he talked to me and to others, and I watched the gradual erosion of a certain reserve that, I suppose, was built within him over years of conscientious work in the civil service. It appeared to me that he had long felt an obligation to display his sense of propriety, to be seen as an upright man, when, in fact, he always was. Now that he was in retirement, the burden of this obligation was lifted. He could laugh freely, and, increasingly, he did. He talked with obvious pleasure to child or man. When he later died, a maid in a neighboring house wept, because, on the few occasions when he had passed her on the road, he had tipped his hat to her and given her a fleeting instant of being thought someone of consequence.

This gradual lessening of reserve showed itself in many ways. But, to me, none were so revealing as the passion he displayed for novels. I had a distinct feeling that earlier he would have proclaimed a novel an entirely frivolous production and would have urged on himself, as on others, the need to have commerce only with "improving" books. This feeling was confirmed by the titles of the books he bought in his younger days. But, after his return to Dublin, he

began to read extensively, sometimes four and five novels
a week. He sat in the armchair before the fireplace in the
living room, holding the book in his right hand, elbow on
knee, using his left hand to turn the pages. Once he began
to read, only the noisiest distraction got through to him.
One night, I had been sitting beside him, talking to my
Aunt Aghna. She knelt in front of him and began to wave
her hand a few inches from his face. She had to continue
doing this for quite a while before he became aware of her
presence. When he finally raised his eyes from the page,
we laughed and explained that we had been talking about
his powers of concentration. He looked puzzled, smiled
briefly, and returned to his reading. A few moments later,
oblivious to our presence, he fought to subdue an emotion
provoked by the misfortune of some character in the novel.

He tended his garden, went to Mass daily, and visited his
friends. In the morning, I often saw him emerging from his
kitchen to the top of the stairs leading to the garden. He
carried a bowl of porridge, which he carefully set down
outside, beside the coal bucket. Then, he returned to the
kitchen, where he read the morning newspaper. Only when
his reading had been completed did he come out to reclaim
his porridge, which by then was a cold, congealed mass, but
which he salted and consumed with no evident revulsion.

Peadar and his bicycle were rarely separated; forty-eight
hours before he died, he went for a fifteen-mile jaunt.
Throughout his life, he loved to cycle, and he was a familiar
sight in the middle of Dublin, going along O'Connell Street.
If it was wet, he had his umbrella, which he raised with one
hand while, with the other, he steered his bicycle amid the
tram lines and the traffic, oblivious to all around him.
Cycling thus in the city with the wind catching his umbrella, a cigarette dangling from his mouth, Peadar was a
fine sight, unaware of the fact that he frequently caused

most of those who saw him moments of sheer panic. Sometimes, as he crossed O'Connell Bridge, a stiff wind would come off the river, and, because he tended to cycle at a moderately slow pace, his bicycle would wobble when he was hit by a sideswipe of the breeze, and his navigation would degenerate into a series of incipient semicircles. He would go on, and buses would swerve, cars would stop, other bicycles would shy away, and policemen on traffic duty would look at him with disbelief. Peadar would pass, and the traffic and its normal routine would resume. Ultimately, Peadar would reach his destination, and, if you asked him whether the streets were crowded, he would reply vaguely, "Oh, yes, there were lots of people." But you knew that he had not really noticed them, that his attention had been riveted on whatever had brought him to town.

Then, one summer afternoon, I was in the big living room when Peadar came in. He was wearing his hat tipped slightly to the left; he had on a blue suit; his trouser legs were held by bicycle clips; and he stood duck-footed, as he always did when talking to someone. His moustache was dark at the center and shaded lighter at the ends.

"What are you doing?" he asked.

"I'm poking through some of the books in the case here," I answered.

"The better ones are gone. It's a pity you can't see them. Ah, well. I'm going for a ride on my bicycle."

He turned and went out. I never saw him again. Three days later we buried his body at Dean's Grange Cemetery. He had died in the hospital of a heart attack. At the cemetery, I remembered, most of all, the grief he had shown at the pain of others. He was dead now. The pain was ours, and it seemed wrong somehow that he was not there to grieve for us and to offer us his inimitable brand of consolation.

6

Granny

We left Peadar at the cemetery, and almost the first thing I noticed afterward was that Granny sang no more. Her silence seemed terrible to me, for she had been singing all her life. She had been highly trained and, indeed, had arranged to continue her studies at La Scala in Milan, but her engagement and marriage had interrupted her career. Nevertheless, Granny had continued to sing for her family and her friends, and, in the years of my boyhood, I had many opportunities to hear and admire her.

Sometimes, when she sang upstairs, I would listen carefully, but my gaze would wander occasionally to some of her paintings on the walls. For Granny had learned to paint with skill and good taste during the years when she had been a student at one of the old-style convent schools in Belgium. Situated at Melsbroek, on the site of the present-day Brussels airport, it had been a medieval structure, with courtyards, Gothic spires, vineyards, and a view of tilled fields and neighboring woods. She had lived and worked with students, some of whom came from circles far above her own, aristocratic circles in France, Austria, and elsewhere. Her roommate had been a Polish princess who had royal monograms on her underwear. In an atmosphere of austere comfort, Granny had written, *"Jesus soit loué"* on the top of every page in her notebook, composed essays, played music, painted, and lived through the passage of happy years.

In the meantime she had kept contact with relatives and friends in Dublin. She had lived briefly in Killiney, about ten miles from the city, and nearly eighty years later she remembered the house distinctly, although she was a small child when she left it. She could recall an older sister who brought her round a spacious garden and helped her pick flowers. She remembered that a Jesuit was living in the house, that he said Mass, and that she was astonished when the servants returned from the drawing room, where Mass had been celebrated, with downcast eyes and their hands clasped around their stomachs.

Granny was a child when her mother died, and, because her father was regularly moved from one area of duty to another, she found herself living in regions as diverse as Glasgow and London. The move to London led to her meeting with Peadar, and, after her marriage, she entered with astonishing zest into a life for which it seemed, at first sight, she could hardly have been prepared. She had ten children; she ran big houses; she entertained; she played and sang; she hired men to carve some of her furniture; and she plunged into her kitchen, where she cooked an abundance of good food for her big family and the constant visitors.

After she had come to Dublin in 1943 and settled upstairs in the house, I could see her every day. I could hear her singing in the kitchen, and, when she tired of singing, she whistled. I came into her kitchen, one morning, to find her at the sink, peeling an onion, which she held at arm's length. The tears were running down her face, but she was whistling an old Irish melody.

She had a great instinct for the moment when the financial resources of a small boy were exhausted. I would hear a "Psst!" or the urgent repetition of my name, and we would meet behind the hall door or somewhere else out of sight. She would slip me some money, and we would go our separate ways, both of us whistling. These secret meetings were part of all my days at home, and the pleasure of them far surpassed the resulting financial gain.

Granny got up early and went to bed late. She hurried about her business, and her energy seemed unlimited. She read all the newspapers, although she was sometimes a week behind. She watched our activities with interest and occasionally indulged her talent for bad puns. Once, when my mother and I were talking about a friend whose travel plans were beset with problems, Granny beamed, yielded, and said, "Why doesn't he say a prayer to Saint Martin of Tours?"

One day past her eightieth birthday, Granny fell and broke her hip. We watched her with dread, and after some weeks, when we saw how she had endured the pain and discouragement of her accident, we began to hope that, perhaps, we might see her home again, bed-ridden to be sure, but with us at least. Later, we hoped she might be able to go around with the aid of a stick. The following year, in her kitchen, she walked up to me and pointed to the stick leaning in the corner. "It's the most useful thing that's come into the house for a long time," she said. "I can use it to reach down the clothes off the rack up there."

In Dublin, where Granny still lives, there is a corruption of the word "old." It is pronounced "oul," as in "foul," or "ould" and connotes advanced age, though not exclusively that, because a child can accuse another of being "an ould cod." The most important aspect of the word is the tone of voice with which it is used. A certain tone indicates that an "ould one" is an aged pest, a blot on the human landscape. But another tone reveals a deep affection for the elderly person to whom it is applied, an esteem born of a happy acquaintance. That is why I find that, when I am asked how my grandmother is, I have a blank moment, until I realize that the inquirer is, of course, referring to "me ould Granny."

7

Night Sounds

When I went to bed at night, my mother pulled the shutters across the window and a flat iron bar, like an arm around a waist, kept them in place. She drew the curtains, too, and, in winter, the room would turn to varying tones of black. With summer and the long days, the light came through the cracks in the shutters, and I knew that, beyond the next house, the high trees, especially the copper beeches and the chestnuts, were catching the last glow of a sky in which the sun had set.

I settled in my bed, not to sleep at first but to listen. My memories of my boyhood are filled with the sounds I used to hear: the talk of my parents in another room; the "ding" of my mother's typewriter when she reached the end of a line (and I knew another of my father's scripts for Radio Eireann was nearly finished); the whirr of a lawnmower on a summer evening; the passage of a bus, which evoked a buzz from a slightly loose windowpane in our living room; the distant train going to Dalkey and Bray and farther south; the voices of neighbors, though they were too far away to be understood; a sudden laugh; and, one night, a scuffle and a cry of terrible fear.

From farther away—from the Liffey and the docks—would come the whistle and the "toot" of small boats and the deep half-muffled "boom" of a large cargo ship that had cast off and was steaming past the lights and the cranes and the sheds. On the nights when fog came off the sea, over the bay and across toward the city, a marvelous pattern of sounds would form: bells clanging along the harbor, sirens blasting high and low, foghorns blowing on their buoys, and one of them, in particular, that came to life when the fog was thickest and sounded like a sheep that had awakened with the tones of a cow.

At Christmas, the carolers would come, and I would be able to hear them making their way along the neighboring roads and stopping to sing under the lamps. There would be a knock at our front door, which someone would quickly open. There would be low voices, the rattle of a money box, and then the closing of the door, and the carols would fade into the wind and the night.

Or upstairs my Aunt Ite would go to the piano, and, after what seemed an unending delay with the practice of her scales, she would move on to Chopin or Debussy. Sometimes, while she played, Granny would sing, and the pleasure of listening to her was mingled with the regret that there was no means of hearing the full glory of her voice as it must have been thirty years earlier.

From the room over mine, a room twice the width of my own, there would come the scrape of chairs, the passage of feet, and the music of a record dimmed behind a roar of laughter. I would hear the laugh of my grandfather, a lingering, baritone laugh held at a single note, textured with the pleasure and amusement he so easily passed on to those with him. I knew then they were sitting around the fire, and the white marble mantelpiece, and the huge mirror.

Out of these sounds and into the darkness would come the memory of others. The memory of a night when suddenly, before my bedtime, the fog came. A bus was stranded behind the church at the end of the road, and my father sent me to find out if the driver and conductor needed anything. I walked slowly, listening to the gathering strength of the foghorns and the sirens and the bells, and, when I reached the bus, the men were sitting with trays of soup and sandwiches that neighbors had brought out to them.

"We're all right, son," said the driver, and he laughed. "We have to stay with the bus, and, if we have to sleep the night with her, sure, can't we claim overtime."

That same night, hundreds of Dubliners emerged into the murk from theaters. Some began to trudge north and believed themselves to be going south. Some wandered in circles around O'Connell Street and adjacent areas. Buses and cars stood silent and abandoned. The fog got thicker, and the lights began to fade, and then came the rescuers— inmates of the asylum for the blind in Drumcondra, tapping their way into O'Connell Street. They collected lost legions of Dubliners and organized them into groups with a common destination. They brought them home, gathering strays as they went and giving courage to those who had lost all sense of direction. When their mission was done, they made their way back to the asylum.

Into the darkness of my room came, too, the memory of

gaiety at Christmas, when my parents, my brother, and I joined the rest of the family for dinner in that room overhead. We usually ate at six o'clock or six-thirty, and the long mahogany table was covered with a starched white linen cloth, which had elaborate designs on it. In the middle of the table were candles, and the light gleamed on the silverware, on the cut glass, and along the dark red flanks of the wine bottles. When everyone had gathered, the shadows danced up the long walls to the high ceiling, with its carved molding. There were the old heavy picture frames, the bookcase in the corner, the armchairs. Into the midst of all this, Granny and my aunts brought the food: a roast turkey, a ham, stuffing, vegetables, potatoes, and much else besides. The dishes were passed while Peadar sharpened his knife on a whetstone and then began to carve the turkey. The dishes circulated, and in front of each of us would appear a mound of food. We were encouraged by Peadar and Granny to start eating, to enjoy it, and to be sure to have plenty more. After this round, Granny disappeared into the kitchen and came back a moment later with a platter of plum pudding, which she herself had made and, indeed, had been making for many days before Christmas. Brandy had been poured over it and set on fire, and, as she came in, the blue flame was on the point of fading out. As the pudding was dished up, there were pleas for "just a little" and "only a tiny bit," and the dishes came back with big slabs of the pudding, on which we put Granny's brandy sauce. In the background there was music.

When all the food had been consumed and all the toasts offered, the dishes were cleared and washed, and then everyone gathered around the fire. There was more talk and music, and people became drowsy, and at last it was time for me and my brother to go downstairs to bed. Once, after we had said goodnight to everyone, we emerged from the warmth of the house and the food and the fun to find that snow had fallen, and the light from the street lamps spread over the snowflakes borne along by the wind.

I lay another night and listened to the footsteps and the moving of chairs overhead, and I noticed that there were no laughs, while outside my door were whispers and the sound of a car arriving. It was the doctor, and, after a while, I heard him go again. Ruaidhri, my uncle, but only a few years older than I was, was seriously ill. The lowered tones and the silent pauses reflected the thought we all had—that a blight had fallen on the house. But, a year later, he was well again and a new sound came to our house, the roar of his motorcycle, and with it came the days when he took me with him on trips to the Dublin mountains, where the wind filled my ears and our echoes trailed behind us.

There were the nights, too, when I lay and listened to the rain. It fell on the trees in the garden, and in spring, when the leaves were fresh, the rainfall was a gentle patter. In autumn, when the leaves had curled and were about to fall, the rain would hiss faintly. Sometimes, a gale would come, and I would listen to the whistle of the wind outside, and I could catch the sound of the sea. Once the tide ran so high that it came over the walls and spilled down the road past the house, so that Ruaidhri, who had been out late that night, had to walk home with his shoes off and his trouser legs rolled up.

But, one night, the sounds outside became queerly muffled, and I could not imagine what had happened. I jumped out of bed in the dark, raised the iron arm off the shutters, and peered out. Heavy snow was falling.

8

Auntie Maggie's Farm

During the war years, my mother sometimes took a day off and went to visit an aunt who lived outside Drogheda, about thirty-five miles north of Dublin. I was always taken along, and we traveled on one of the cream and blue buses of the old Great Northern Railway Line. The trip usually took about an hour and a half, and, when we reached Drogheda, we transferred to a second bus for the remainder of the journey.

Sometimes Peadar came along with us. One day, when he, my mother, and I were passing through Drogheda, a town he knew very well because he had been born not far from it, Peadar pointed to an old building that looked more like a mill than a private dwelling house, and he began to tell my mother that, in that house, at the turn of the century, had been installed the first known overhead shower in Drogheda. There was a spacious cubicle with plenty of room in which to move about, and the water was obtained by pulling a chain hanging from above, more or less in the same way as with old-style toilets. Peadar went on to tell the story of a young lady who decided to use the shower, having been invited by the owners to do so. She stepped in and first washed her hair. When the moment came for her to rinse, she was blinded by soap and reached up to find the chain, without success. She began to move around, groping over her head, but her hand found nothing. Eventually, a helpful male voice came from above: "If ye'd just move about two feet to yer right, ma'am, ye'll be able to reach it." Peadar and my mother laughed, and I'm not at all sure that I was supposed to have heard.

The streets in the middle of Drogheda are filled with reminders of the town's past, of which part was the massacre of the population by Oliver Cromwell. In the central church, in a case with a glass door, is the blackened, shriveled head of Oliver Plunkett, an archbishop who was hanged, drawn, and quartered in London during earlier, evil days.

As we waited for the second bus, which would take us out to Auntie Maggie's farm, we would sometimes look over the quay wall at the River Boyne, emerging there after crossing a valley, which in spring is a paradise of tall trees, flowering shrubs, and the rich stirrings of fertile soil. The bus took us along the river for three or four miles, then turned in and continued until it was time to alight at the entrance to a road that went straight for about a quarter of a mile. At the end of this road was Auntie Maggie's house, a long, single-story building that in those days had a thatched roof. There was a small garden at the front and a sun porch. Around at the back were two rectangular yards, each of them lined with sheds and outbuildings where everything from cars to chickens was kept. We were welcomed at the back door by Auntie Maggie, a small woman who became increasingly bent as the years went on, until finally she could support herself only by using a walking stick. She was Peadar's sister, and she had long been a widow. In the surrounding district, she had many sisters and nephews who lived and worked on farms that bore names such as Ganderstown, Crucetown, and Hill of Rath. (I was a teenager before I discovered, sadly and with the collapse of cherished images, that the last was not the Hill of "Wrath.") Her own farm was Ballyfaddock in the parish of Termonfeckin, and, from her sunporch, she could look across hedges and fields to the tall spire of the church and the trees rising below it.

After having lunched inside and while my mother and Auntie Maggie and Peadar chatted and talked and exchanged news, I hastened out, for there was much to do. In the farther yard were huge haysheds, and it was a constant delight to go out to play in these. I used to inspect the farm machinery, and, every time we came, it seemed that something new had been added. There were the animals to see. Sometimes I helped with the feeding of the calves. And there were the milking machines, which always fascinated me. They were clipped onto the cows, and in due course foaming buckets of milk appeared. I was told that they were labor-saving devices, that the old-style farmer who sat on a stool to milk by hand was a thing of the past. I was not completely convinced of this as I watched the elaborate preparations for the milking and the careful cleaning of the machinery that was necessary when the job was done.

The man who ran the farm for Auntie Maggie was her

grandson Jim, and the high point in many of my trips to
the farm was a ride with Jim on the tractor, where I was
permitted to sit on his lap and to steer. Then, sooner or
later, and with mixed feelings, I would visit the "facilities."
I had never seen anything like it before. One had to go
from the house down a long, straight path bordered on
one side by a tall hedge and on the other by an orchard. At
the end of the path was a little green house, and inside it
was a bench, on one side of which there was a pile of old
newspapers, and in the middle of the bench was a hole with
a cover on it. Nothing in my life in Dublin had prepared
me for such an institution, and, indeed, the only one I have
seen since was a companionable two-holer in a museum.

On the way back from this outdoor toilet, and as a kind
of reward for the long trip that had been necessary, there
was a low tree from which I always plucked some leaves,
for they had a marvelous sweet fragrance. I have never
been able to find out the name of it, but a branch taken
back to Dublin and kept in my room was a reminder, for
days after, of the delight that I had experienced during my
trip to Ballyfaddock.

One of the purposes of our visits to Ballyfaddock was to
get supplies of butter and eggs to supplement the wartime
ration in the city. In the dairy at Auntie Maggie's was a
butter churn, shaped like a beer barrel, that rested on a
raised platform. There was a handle at one side like the
crank handle used on old-fashioned cars, and it made the
entire barrel revolve. From inside came the sloshing sounds
of milk—sounds that became gradually thicker and slurred
as the butter formed. Then someone would scoop out the
butter, salt it, and beat it with wooden paddles. Afterward,
it was wrapped in greaseproof paper, some of it packed
away for my mother to carry back to the city. This butter
was always a delicacy in our house during the war years, as

were the eggs and flour that Auntie Maggie gave my mother.

At the end of a long day, the time came to return to Dublin, and I was always sad to leave. The promise that we would come again at a later date was not much comfort. We walked to the end of the road and waited for the bus that would take us back to Drogheda and on home. Sometimes, we stopped off in Drogheda to visit friends or relatives of Mother's. Only one such visit sticks in my mind. We went to a cloistered convent in which one of my mother's cousins was a nun. With astonishment and awe I followed my mother into a large living room that was divided in half by a paneled wall about three feet high, this wall being joined to the ceiling by a grille. On the other side of the partition, the cousin appeared in white robes and with a black veil. The whispered talk seemed a little strained. My mother, who had brought a gift, perhaps a box of sweets, put it on a revolving shelf, which spun round to face the inside of the grille, from which place the nun could retrieve it and turn the shelf back around to face us. There could be no shaking of hands, no physical contact.

The first time I visited this place, I was astounded by everything I saw, and, a few days later, in school, I discussed it with a desk mate who had also visited such a convent. When I asked him what happened when one of the nuns died, I was told that the corpse was put on the revolving shelf and handed out to a waiting undertaker, to be taken thence for burial.

I do not remember that we visited this convent often. Usually, there was little delay in Drogheda as we waited to catch the second bus, and, by the time the bus had reached the city and come down by the Liffey, the day was nearly over. Night was drawing on when we neared home, and I was well ready for bed.

9

Sandymount National School

"Are ya sorry the war is over?"

"No, I'm not sorry," I said, "I'm glad."

"Take him away," said the tallest of them. And the group of boys from the sixth class, the highest class at school, grabbed me and led me across the yard. I was brought over to the water fountain and my head was stuck under a tap. But the day was nice, the sun was out, and I did not particularly mind the fact that I had had a shower. While I was drying off, I saw another of my schoolmates dragged across as I had been. He too was put under the tap; he too emerged shaking drops of water from his eyebrows; and I learned from him that the answer he had given was the opposite of mine. So it apparently made no difference where one stood on this important question.

This was in Sandymount National School, which was near my home, and I started there when I was seven. It was not my first school experience. I had not been to kindergarten, but, because my father was a schoolteacher, I had sometimes gone into his class to sit for an hour. My mother would take me over to the school; my father would sit me with one of the boys in his room; and I would take part in the ritual of the class. I sat with my pencil and my notebook and was presented with arithmetic problems as were all the others, and, because I could see no particular point to the exercise, I leaned over to my neighbor, copied his answers, and settled back to enjoy myself.

So, when I came to Sandymount, the routine was already a familiar one. The classrooms were small, and we sat at double desks, with bench seats, and there was a little compartment under the desk top in which a school bag or a lunch or a clandestine piece of chocolate could be stored. In the middle of each desk was an inkwell for use with our wooden pens.

The first book we used showed on its opening page two monkeys sitting at a table. Each monkey wore a bib; the table was covered with a linen cloth; there was a tea set; and the monkeys were daintily engaged in the exercise of enjoying an afternoon meal. Underneath was an attempted poem, which ran as follows:

> No one knows and no one cares
> What the king of the monkeys wears.
> But we who are Irish should always be tidy
> When we sit down to tea.

I think it must have been at that point that I began to lose interest in the school's curriculum. My memory of exactly what we did is extremely vague. I know we studied writing, arithmetic, and algebra and that we read texts in English and Irish and had classes in Irish history, in geography, and in singing. Each week, we all learned a new song, which we rehearsed over and over again. But, apart from that, my recollection of the scholastic activities of the National School is quite uncertain.

The things that do stick in my memory had little to do with study, but I did enjoy writing essays, and I remember one essay I wrote of which I was particularly proud. I handed it in for correction during a fateful visit by the school inspector. Coming from a family of teachers, which included one inspector, I was well aware of what a visit by an inspector could mean in a school. I was not for a moment deceived by the jovial, friendly smiles of both inspector and inspected, for it was not the students who were being inspected; it was the teachers. The inspector would come in and talk about the weather and look jovial and smile at the students and rub his hands and say, "Well, well, well," and go through all the motions of putting a class at its ease. Having done that, he would then turn to the work of the day.

I remember one of these inspectors coming in. A tall, white-haired man, he wore a tweed sports jacket, and he took over our teacher's chair up in front of the class and began to read our essays. He invited me to sit beside him and said genially that he had just read my essay, that he liked it very much, but that there were a few things that needed to be fixed up. He pointed to one sentence where I had described a small boy to whom something had happened, who cried so hard that a great pool of tears lay on the floor all around him. The inspector looked at me.

"Don't you think that that's just a little bit of an exaggeration?" he asked.

"No," I replied.

"Oh, come on, now," he said, "whoever heard of a little boy crying so much that there was a whole pool of tears all around him?"

So, because he was the inspector, and also because he was over six feet tall, I yielded the point. But I was not convinced.

In my second year in Sandymount School, we were shifted to a new classroom. This had once been a hall, and it was quite spacious. The desks were all lined up, there was a big mullioned window at the back, and underneath it was a clock, which we watched, particularly as it moved toward the blessed hour of release. There were some old cupboards, and, in one of these, the teacher kept his books and his pencils and his chalk and his supply of nibs for our pens and all the other paraphernalia of his job.

He also kept there whatever instrument he was currently using for purposes of punishment. Sometimes it was a stick; sometimes it was a leather strap. He was not ferocious in the use of these, and the strap, although it made a great noise when it descended on an outstretched hand, did not hurt nearly as much as the stick. I think it was the noise of the strap that outraged us all, and, hence, my career in the school was periodically marked by a surreptitious entry into the master's closet when nobody else was around. I had discovered a means of opening the closet without having to open the lock, and I would steal the stick or strap or whatever instrument of torture was there. For a few days he would be helpless. He could not punish anybody, except with an occasional wallop over the back of the ear, but, eventually, he would come in with a new stick or strap with which to beat us.

Although I was not greatly interested in my studies, I must have been a reasonably competent student, because I was entrusted regularly with the job of going to the school down the road, and also to the neighboring classrooms, to bring around circulars that had to be signed, and this afforded me happy relief. Although I did all the jobs entrusted to me quite conscientiously, I took my time about them. I learned quickly that a job well done is not necessarily a job done in a hurry. "Hurry," in this case, meant a speedy return to the classroom, where I would have to sit and carry on with, perhaps, some arithmetic or some geography or some new chapter in Irish history, which, at the time, interested me not one bit.

The students in the class came mostly from the area of Ringsend, which at that time was fairly heavily populated with very poor families who were crowded together into slums, which have long since disappeared. The children from Ringsend came from various backgrounds. Some of their fathers worked as stevedores down at the harbor; some of them were actually sailors, but most were casual laborers whose work was dictated by the nature of what was going on at the harbor. Among the schoolboys there were the usual cabals, the usual gangs, the usual games and pranks.

One afternoon, while sitting at my desk, I was slipped a matchbox. When I opened it I found a note that said, "The Raven Gang will get you." It was then one hour before the end of the school day, and my problem was to find out, first, how big the Raven Gang was and, second, what I could do to avoid it. What it was going to "get" me for, I do not remember now. But the remaining hour was spent in lining up a rival gang, and, when school ended, the Raven Gang had stationed members on all the paths that led from the school. But they had not reckoned with the fact that a second gang would now appear. While the two gangs fought, I contentedly packed my bag and headed on home.

Our teacher was a kindly and a good man, and, if he occasionally yelled at us, it was because we deserved it. If he occasionally left a student with very sore hands, it was not because he had lost his temper or committed any injustice. Indeed, the worst punishments we saw in that classroom were meted out not by the teacher but by an occasional irate father, who would come in from Ringsend to find out why a son of his was not doing better.

I remember one wet afternoon, as we were sitting there in class, a man burst in on us. He was a docker from Ringsend who had been out of work for several weeks. Time was heavy on his hands, his patience was running thin, and he came to find out why his son Matty was causing so much trouble. Matty was, indeed, a troublemaker. He rarely did any of the work he was supposed to do. The teacher frequently complained about him. And Matty was not overly interested in mending his ways, but we all admired him for various reasons. I admired him because he went regularly to the Regal Cinema in Ringsend. The Regal is no longer there, but, when I was eight, nine, and ten it was a flea pit down beside the harbor. Children could go in for four pennies. I went once, and I could never forget it, because the place was packed with children and the noise of shouting and screaming and kicking and fighting was so intense, there was such bedlam all around, that none of the dialogue on the screen could be heard. I admired Matty because he went there once a week. I do not know where he got the four pennies to pay his admission fee, and I suspect he did not acquire them legitimately. But Matty would come on Monday morning and tell us of the latest film he had seen. Not only did his account of the film enthrall us, but so did his description of the audience. I have never seen anyone who could imitate so well the act whereby a man stands up in the middle of a flea pit and is finally no longer able to restrain himself from scratching. Matty used to tell us about the film, about the heroine, about the actions of the hero, and all these tales kept us enthralled during the dreary hours when we had to do such unpleasant things as learn the catechism or read our history books, or do some addition or division or multiplication.

But, this afternoon, justice caught up with Matty. His father burst in. He had a peaked cap on, and it was slung at a rakish angle over one eye. I suspect he must have been drinking. He asked the teacher if Matty had been behaving well recently, if he had been doing his work. The teacher admitted that Matty had not. Matty was called from his desk, and as the boy walked to the back of the room, his father took off his belt. It must have been at least four inches wide. He grabbed Matty by one hand; then, he began to strap him around and around and around the back of the room while Matty screamed and the teacher looked on, silent and obviously appalled. The rest of us sat at our desks, chilled and numb.

Another student was a little boy called Sidney. His father was a very short man, and Sidney had six brothers. He, too, rarely did any work and was often in trouble. He brought in comic books and other distractions to help him through the day. And, because he was not overly clever, he was almost always caught with whatever he had brought in. So he had to be punished. But what I remember principally about Sidney was the fact that he was a sort of walking obituary column. Sidney knew about every death in the neighborhood, and sometimes he would come and tell us that he had gone into a house and looked at the corpse. When we came into class, we looked to Sidney to tell us all about the latest death in the area.

The first time I ever saw a corpse was when Sidney came in one day and told us that, down the road from the school, an old man had just died and all the children could come and pray for him. He led us to the house, and we all trembled with excitement. It was a small house with low ceilings. There were two floors, but a man six feet tall would have had to bend in any one of the rooms. We climbed a staircase into a room that had been darkened, and there in the bed lay the body of the old man. The yellow blinds had been pulled down, and the gloomy light seemed to take its hue from the waxen face of the dead man. A single housefly hovered over his mouth and nose. We knelt and said a prayer for him, gazed with the curiosity of children, and then withdrew. Sidney felt very proud that he had added to our education.

Another of the students was an unfortunate boy named Kavanagh, who had a terrible stammer, and we always agonized for him. Not many laughed at him, because it was so obviously a painful affliction. We used to discuss possible cures for it. We were once told that a remedy for stammering was to hold a penny very tightly in one's hand; the contact with the penny would be sufficient to produce speech. One day, when Kavanagh was called on in class to answer a question and, as usual, got completely tied up in his words, and stumbled and stammered and gasped, I whipped out a penny, slipped it into his palm, and urged him to squeeze it. He got completely confused. He pressed on the penny. The teacher saw what was going on and quietly told me to leave him alone. Kavanagh got more excited. He dropped the penny, and, instead of being able to utter a few syllables, he got nothing out at all. So we looked around sadly for another sure remedy.

One day, I was called out with half a dozen others, and we were told that we were to become altar boys. My career was brief and relatively undistinguished. We were brought into the sacristy of the church, and there, once a week, for some time, we learned the Latin responses to the Mass. Each of us had to have a soutane and an alb. We were taught not only to respect the Latin responses of the Mass but also to allow for the fact that individual celebrants might have their quirks and special needs.

We all particularly feared one of the curates of the parish, and we hesitated to serve him. He was a quick-tempered man who liked his Masses short and speedy. He had no time for the solemn pronunciation of the ancient Latin formulas. He delivered the prayers with a business-like efficiency (especially during the weekday Masses), which served to remind us that, if he were a bit slower, his breakfast—at that moment being cooked in his house across the road—would get cold. He was also a man who liked to give sermons that were brief and to the point. He was distant and demanding toward altar boys. One lesson we were taught during our training was to watch out lest some priest might omit a portion of the Mass, but we were also told that, if we discovered a priest doing so, we would have to be very careful as to how we would bring the fact to his attention. For there was the case of the feared curate, who was approached by one of the altar boys in the group ahead of us. The unfortunate boy had come to him during Mass to tell him that he had left out an important bit. The priest turned on the altar and barked back, "Who the hell's saying this Mass anyway, you or me?"

After we had learned the Latin responses, we were allowed to take part in Benediction, which meant taking a candle and appearing on the altar with the other boys while the service was in progress. The most favored among us was allowed to have the thurible. This was an honor for which we all vied. It meant that one stood at the center of the altar, with a little brazier, which was swung back and forth rhythmically. The important point was to avoid swinging it too far, to prevent hot coals from flying out and burning the carpet or some neighboring altar boy.

What pleased me most as an altar boy were the priests who paid no attention to me. There were those who came and mumbled the opening formulas as fast as they could, and whether I responded or not was a matter of indifference to them. The important thing was for me to make some sort of noise, thus giving the impression that I was responding. The duty that most appealed to me was that of ringing the church bell when a funeral took place.

The procedure at a funeral was somewhat like this: The body in the coffin would be brought to the church in the evening and left overnight. The following morning, there would be Mass. At the end of Mass, the celebrant would retire to his house and have his breakfast. After this, he would reappear and go with the hearse and the mourning cars out to the cemetery, where he would lead the prayers and perform the last rites for the dead. The crux of the matter here was the time between the end of Mass and the reappearance of the priest, especially the curate, who obviously liked either to linger over his breakfast or to have a big one. This interval would be filled by the slow ringing of the bell, while the coffin was put into the hearse outside and the mourners gathered and talked sadly among themselves.

The church in Sandymount had a bell tower, with the long rope inside, and the task that I particularly enjoyed was hanging on the rope and swinging on the bell, so there would be one long mournful bong and then a suitable interval would be allowed to elapse until it was time to ring again.

But there is a blank in my memory as to when or why I ceased to be an altar boy. I can only recall that, one time, my soutane split from end to end. Perhaps it was a sign of something or other.

IO

"Mitching" and Other Sports

One day, when I was coming out of school, I saw a printed notice on a billboard near the gates. It said, "AMERICAN TEA SALE." It gave the following Monday as the date, and it proclaimed that the sale would take place in the school. I brought this piece of information home to my mother. I had no idea what an American tea sale was, nor do I yet know. Certainly, it could not have meant a sale of American tea, or rather of teabags, because the teabag is still regarded by most Irishmen as an outrage against nature. But I informed my mother that the sale was taking place, and I told her that it was to be in the school, and I conveyed that this could only mean that the school would be closed for the day. And my mother said, "Well, that's very handy because, on Monday, I want to go to Balrothery to see Mr. Stack. You can come along with me."

So I mitched, or played truant, that Monday, and a glorious, marvelous day it proved to be. I prepared for it well on the preceding Friday. The teacher had left the class for a moment, and, while he was gone, I slipped up to the clock and pushed the hand forty minutes ahead. When the teacher came back, he seemed a bit surprised that the time had gone by so quickly, but he had no suspicion of what had really happened and, accordingly, dismissed us. When he came in the following Monday, it was to demand in outrage who had put the clock ahead. One of my classmates proceeded to inform on me, but I was far away.

It was a sunny day; the sky was blue; and we took a bus from Dublin to the small village of Balrothery, twenty-five miles north of Dublin. When we arrived there, the bus stopped on a long stretch of road and we climbed out, and Mr. Stack was waiting to welcome us.

An old friend of Peadar's, he was, by that time, in retirement after a career in the Customs and Excise Service. He had bought this house in Balrothery after his retirement. It was a spacious house and had at least three floors. It had huge rooms. Best of all, it had orchards and a big farmyard attached to it, and, on the day we arrived, some of the first spring crops were ready—lettuce and tomatoes and the like. It was too early yet for the plums and apples and pears that grew in abundance in the orchard. All that day, with the sun shining and the sky blue, I played and explored this marvelous house and garden. When I had tired of the orchards, I moved into a barn packed with straw and had the fun of climbing up to the second floor and throwing myself off, tumbling head first into the straw and somersaulting and rolling down to the bottom. It was with the greatest reluctance that I went into the house to have lunch, and I bolted whatever food was given me and ran out again. There were trees all around; there were fields that had turned to that fresh, ripe green that comes so slowly with the spring. Later, back in the house, I found a room piled with old numbers of the *National Geographic Magazine*. I had never seen this magazine before, and I was fascinated by the photographs. I spent a happy hour poking through the old issues and looking at pictures of exotic people and places.

Mr. Stack was a benign and rather serious man who wore a gold watch chain over his middle and had a habit of closing one eye when he explained a point of view. He seemed to have only a slight sense of humor, but he was very polite and extremely kind. He was also getting rather deaf. He had an older sister who lived in North Dakota, and she came back to this wonderful house and, after a few weeks, announced that she was half-dead with the cold. So Mr. Stack sold the house and the land and bought himself a house in Dublin and installed a central-heating system that made the heat greater than that of a greenhouse on a summer day. The friends who had been accustomed to visiting him cut their calls gradually to brief, sweaty visits. When he had finally gotten the place thoroughly warmed up, he sent word to his sister that the house was ready for her. She came back and spent a few months there and then got tired of it. She headed back to North Dakota, and Mr. Stack spent the rest of his days in the house in Dublin, overheated and visited by fewer and fewer friends.

He used to come out to our house often, mainly to talk to Peadar. They were both expert gardeners, and they liked to discuss the subject at length. They spent two happy years building a compost heap, speculating on its possibilities, and analyzing what they should put into it next. Finally, Mr. Stack reached the point where he could hear nothing, but he still came to the house, and, because he was an old friend, he was made very welcome, though nobody could communicate with him. He continued this way for many years, and then, one morning, he had come out of his house and was halfway across the street when he failed to hear a car that was coming up fast. He was knocked down and killed.

But that was still in the future. He obviously loved the house in Balrothery, and he cultivated the garden with skill. All that wonderful sunny day I played and explored and gamboled around in the back yard and the farmyard and the barn and the house and the fields behind. At the end of the evening, Mr. Stack brought us down to the bus, which delivered us back to Dublin.

Next day, when I went to school, my teacher was waiting for me. He asked me if it were true that I had put the clock forward on Friday. I said it was, and, as I knew well that I could be severely punished for having done so, I pointed out that I had gone into a church to say a prayer and that the clock there had shown precisely the same time as the one in the school after I had put it ahead. The church time must have been accurate. My teacher seemed to accept this argument, and I managed to escape punishment this time. I was then asked to explain my absence of the previous day. I did so very simply. My mother had had to go to Balrothery to get some things, and, of course, she had to have help, and so she had brought me along.

In those years, too, I engaged briefly and ingloriously in the sports that were part of the school life. In particular, I joined one of the hurling teams. Hurling is a game that, when properly played, can be extremely exciting. (One holds a stick rather like a hockey stick, except that the

lower end is wide enough to hold the ball. One is allowed
to pick the ball off the ground with the stick and run down
the field, bouncing the ball on the stick. The stick may be
raised above one's shoulders to pluck a ball from the air
or to drive it on its way toward the goal.) As played by
experts, the sport is a delight to watch, but, when played
by people like me, it can be rather disorganized. For a brief
period, I played with a school team. We used to go down
to Ringsend Park, where we practiced. I cannot recall contributing anything spectacular to any of the games in
which I joined. My principal memory is of a day on which
a personal animosity between myself and a member of the
opposing team was worked out skillfully in center field.
We were facing each other; others were coming at us;
everyone was tackling everybody else trying to get the ball.
My opponent finally came to the conclusion that, because
he could offer no really effective action in the play, he
might as well use his time to some personal advantage. He
reached out and stuck his hurling stick between my legs. I
tripped and fell on my face. Having dusted myself off, I
decided to wait for an appropriate opportunity to get even.
It came a few minutes later, when we were once again all
massed in center field. This time he was closer to the ball,
indeed so close that he looked as if he might get it and be
able to make a contribution to the game. I pushed my way
as near to him as I could, reaching the hurling stick across,
and took a swipe at the ball, making sure I caught him
across the shins. This disabled him for the next fifteen or
twenty minutes, and the game went on.

In the classroom, there were many ways in which we
whiled away the tedium of the hours: We sent notes around
to each other; we exchanged spitballs. A particularly effective form of attack was to take bits of paper, dip them in

the inkwell, and then make a rubber catapult, or slingshot, and send them flying over at an opponent on the other side of the classroom. Sometimes we brought in comics and read them; sometimes we brought in books. We also had games. One was called jackstones. It was really very simple. One had only to take a pile of small pebbles, hold them in the palm of the hand, toss them up, turn the hand over, and try to catch the pebbles between the fingers. There were elaborate rules connected with this game, but the important thing was that, if you played it in class and misjudged, the pebbles would fall on the floor, making a great deal of noise and, therefore, attracting attention to oneself. So, the game, offering the excitement of the risk of being caught, was a very popular one with us.

At another season of the year, when the chestnuts were ripe, we went around the neighborhood climbing trees and combing the area underneath them for fallen chestnuts. We would take one, bore a hole in the middle, put a piece of string perhaps twelve inches long through the hole, tie a knot so that the chestnut would hang on the string, and then go around challenging each other's "conkers." The game consisted quite simply of holding up one's own chestnut while the opponent took a swipe at it with his. If he missed, then it was your turn, and the object of the whole game was to see whose chestnut could split that of the opponent. Then it became a question of having chestnuts that had split ten, fifteen, twenty other chestnuts. There would be championships in which the holder of a chestnut that had split twenty-four others would be pitted against the holder of a chestnut that had split thirty, and so on.

There were other distractions, too. One day a small boy named Kennedy came in. He had been down to the docks. An American ship had come in, and young Kennedy had been able to acquire some chewing gum. From our film-going we knew what it was, but we had never actually seen it. There was great envy of Kennedy because he had gone a step ahead of us in this important matter. So we made bargains with him, and, as a result, an entire afternoon was spent while the one wad of chewing gum was passed from hand to hand and, thus, from mouth to mouth. Most of the class tried it out. I was one of the few who declined, with thanks.

And then, suddenly, it was over and six years had passed and we were graduating members of the senior class. The talk was of what we would do when we left. For some, like myself, there was secondary school ahead, and after that the university. For others, it was the end of the road. Matty and Sidney and Kavanagh, and many of their friends, would move out to work on the docks, to be messenger boys, to become apprentices to carpenters. Within seven or eight years, they would marry and have their own families. I and some of my classmates had a long summer holiday before us, and, as we left Sandymount School, we had our first real inkling of how people often have to go their separate ways.

Spinsters and Spinnets

When I was nine or ten, I was enrolled in a school of music, where each week I tried to learn to play the piano. The school was in one of a row of Georgian houses on Harcourt Street. There was a very high, wide door with an elaborate, fan-shaped leaded window overhead, and the doorstep carried a shoe-scraper. You went up a wide staircase. On each landing was a marble statue that had been carefully sculpted. The second and third floors were occupied by the school. It was run by an elderly lady to whom I was introduced on my first day. She was tall, bespectacled, and bundled up. Around her neck hung a fox skin, with a snout hanging over either shoulder and beady eyes gleaming. She smiled benignly at me or at any other student.

The secretary was at work. She had a haircut in the style of the 1920's, and she, too, was a spinster, and aging. She worked in a room occupied by one of the teachers, and she sat at a mahogany bureau on which stood a tall ink stand and a long-handled pen. In the winter, she had big fur boots on and she wore her coat over several layers of cardigans. On her left hand she wore a glove, and on the right she wore a mitten that reached to her knuckles. The bare portion of this hand, from the knuckles to the fingertips, was invariably blue with the cold. She used to plug in a little stove, which she kept beside her boots, and it may have warmed her boots, but very little else.

In each of the rooms there was a piano, of course. The ceilings were high and had elaborate moldings. The rooms were partitioned off by folding doors, so that one could imagine them open in bygone days to form a big Georgian ballroom, with dancing and long dresses and gay talk.

When we came in, each of us would usually arrive a few minutes before the lesson, would go into the appropriate room, where there was a chair, and would sit in the chair and wait his turn. In the winter, one's breath would turn to steam as he waited.

My teacher was middle-aged, the only one in the institution who was married, and there must have been some feeling in the place that marriage and music did not go together, because she had to teach under her maiden name. I was there a year before I discovered that she had a husband and a growing family. She was very nice, but she had to be a disciplinarian, of course. She started me off on my music. I bought my books, and I learned little pieces and played brief tunes, and she would write instructions in pencil at the top of my music. She would write "H.T.," which meant I was to practice "hands together" for the following week, or "R.H." (right hand) or "L.H." (left hand), and I began to learn to play compositions with titles such as "The Merry Peasant" and "The Country Dancers." She was very firm about my having to practice, and, when I went home, I was fairly dutiful at first, but then the days came when I had to be reminded that it was time to prepare my lessons. This reminder became increasingly necessary throughout that first year.

Then, in my second year, I was promoted, and, in addition to having the same teacher, I also went in on Saturday morning to study musical theory with another lady. A whole group of us would sit around a carved mahogany table, and the lady would sit at a piano and play chords. We were supposed to identify the chords and the keys, and we would go on from there to other aspects of musical theory, which I have completely forgotten. They did not register. Then, I had to buy staff paper and write out some exercises to be handed in. I had no idea what it was all about, but I filled out all the spaces, and received the thing back the following week with the comment "Not understood," which was nicely put; whether it meant that the teacher had not understood what I was doing or that I had not understood what she was doing was not clear.

This was how we operated, week in, week out, and sometimes the regular trip there became something of a burden. One evening, toward the end of May, I had a lesson at 6:30 or 7:00, and, as I went through town, I passed by Stephen's Green, and, of course, Stephen's Green is marvelous in May: The trees are all fresh; the flower beds are full; the grass is new and green; the sun is out. I had my music, and all of a sudden I felt a desire for rebellion. I stuffed the music in my pocket, and I spent the whole evening wandering around Stephen's Green, looking at the flowers and sitting under the trees and lying on the grass and enjoying the sunshine while it lasted and it was pure pleasure—pleasure compounded by the fact that it was illicit.

Of course, the following week I had to offer an explanation for my absence, and I decided that anything but the truth was called for. I decided that, because I had to spin a tale, it might as well be a fanciful one. I do not remember all the details of it, but it involved my having to fly at short notice out of Dublin airport to assist in some kind of dramatic production somewhere in the south of Ireland. I drew heavily upon a description of our landing at Shannon and being swept off by cars to our destination. It must have been a most impressive tale, because there was no question but that this was a valid excuse. Of course, one of the disadvantages was, you could not try that kind of thing too often.

My music lessons went on for a few years. At one stage, I was even thought to be sufficiently advanced to play at the annual Feis Ceoil. It used to be held then—and, I think, still is—in a hall near Leinster House. One plays a number of set pieces; there is also a sight test; and an adjudicator sitting at a little table at the back, with a cup of tea beside him and lots of notes, writes down comments about you. My name was quite far down the list, and a paralyzing dread came over me as I sat in the back and awaited my turn to appear on the stage. My performance was obviously not too impressive, because I got no mention in the contest, but I did get a report from the adjudicator, implying I had a good deal to learn. He was right, of course. But, by then, I was stirred by other interests, and the thought of coming years filled with forays to Harcourt Street proved too much; at last, my father agreed to let me abandon my lessons, which I did without regret.

But I was destined to be subjected once more to an attempt to train me in things musical. When I was a teenager, a lady I knew decided that I could make no headway in social life without some experience in the art of dancing. She took me aside regularly, when we were in a position not to be overheard, and talked to me about the importance of being able to step onto a dance floor with a calm knowledge of how to perform. It took a while to convince me, and then she asked me as a favor to agree to take lessons at a dancing studio she knew, where she would arrange private instruction for me. I agreed to do so, providing it was done in strict secrecy, and the agreement sprang more from the desire to please her than from any visions of success on the ballroom floor.

And so, once a week, for some months, I went to a studio near Stephen's Green. My instructor was the proprietor of the establishment. He was in his fifties, about five feet tall, with horn-rimmed spectacles, a little toothbrush moustache, and a developing paunch. He assured me during the first lesson that *anyone* could become a master of the art of dancing. And, just to prove it, he put on some records, and, when the music got going, he danced alone around the floor of the studio. He waltzed and tangoed and fox-trotted. He swept an imaginary lady in circles around him. He urged me to watch his feet, and I did so with intense concentration.

Then, during the second lesson, he invited me onto the floor and devoted most of twenty minutes to demonstrating how I ought to hold a partner during a dance. "Hold me here; that's where you hold them," he said, and I hesitantly placed the fingers of my left hand on a point somewhere above the pocket of his tweed jacket. Then, he held out his left hand as if he were stopping a bus, and I matched the gesture, and we were all set. "Just a moment, please." He slipped out of my grasp and went over to put on a record. The music was a tango, and we began a more or less rhythmic progress around the room. He counted off the time, and I concentrated on my feet. Through the remainder of the lesson, we circled the floor, while he murmured, "It's quite simple, really," and I tried to discover a formula that would coordinate my feet with the need to move.

This procedure was followed during the next weeks. I held him chastely; he counted out the time; and we occasionally talked about the latest news. I noticed that all his advice was strictly related to deportment, with never a word about the fact that it was a girl I might someday have on my arm when I ventured out in the big world. His wife visited us one day during a lesson, and I quickly understood why his attention was devoted exclusively to the dynamics of dancing. She was at least a foot taller than he was.

When the course of instruction was over, my friend decided that it was time to go to a real dance. She brought me out to a ballroom in Bray one Saturday night. "Nobody will know you there," she said, "so you needn't feel a bit shy." She stood in front of me, hardly more than five feet tall herself. When we began to dance, I realized that ladies' paunches are in a different place, a fact I should have taken into consideration before that. This, combined with the fact that *she* gripped *me* firmly around the waist, left me with a problem of equilibrium for which my dancing master had not provided. The result of it all was that, besides stepping on her toes, I found myself with a regular inclination to topple over.

We stayed for about an hour, and my feet continued to refuse to coordinate with either the music or my partner. Then, I drove her home in her car and did not dance again until five years later, at which time I found that my talents had not deteriorated noticeably.

12

Bird-Watching

At some time in the course of the years when I was in primary school, I acquired an interest in bird-watching. How this enthusiasm was evoked in me I cannot tell. But I do recall that I read with considerable interest a book by a very eminent ornithologist, who pointed out that bird-watching was a pastime in which distinctions of class and society were obliterated—that firemen and cabinet ministers, financiers and street-sweepers were all known to have devoted themselves passionately to this hobby. As a result, my bird-watching days were filled not only with the interest of the occupation itself but also with the hope of encountering some distinguished members of circles in which I did not move. It took me some time to realize, of course, that the writer was an Englishman and that he was talking about his fellow countrymen. In the two or three years when I was an ardent ornithologist, I never once encountered a cabinet minister or a financier, or for that matter a street-sweeper, who zealously hid in marshes to get a view of a female crested grebe or a long-tailed tit.

I had a red notebook in which I kept a diary of the passage of birds and the calls I had heard from neighboring trees or from the shore. I also had a few books that I read very carefully and in which I studied the characteristics of the birds I was likely to see regularly or not at all. The one indispensable instrument of bird-watching, namely, a pair of field glasses, I lacked completely. For a while, I had the use of a pair of opera glasses, and, on the day I got these, I rushed off to see if I could find a bird and study it at closer quarters. Unfortunately, I was to discover that, when I did eventually come within range of a bird and focus on it, the creature was ringed by a rainbow that made identification almost impossible. Also, the bird was brought probably no more than two feet closer by the use of the glasses.

But at least I was enthusiastic, and my parents encouraged me to persevere. Because I lived near the sea, much of my time at this stage was spent watching shore birds. Where Sandymount Strand takes its first turn toward forming what will eventually become the right arm of Dublin Bay, there was a corner particularly favored by birds and lovers. This corner was bounded by a wall behind which there was a railway line, and I would frequently creep inside the wall until I was satisfied that I was within close range of a dunlin or a sandpiper. I would slowly raise my head, taking the greatest possible care to make no noise, and my eyes would come level with the top of the wall. I would freeze for a moment, listening intently, and then I would raise my head up. Instead of a redshank, I frequently encountered the angry stares of a courting couple. To insist that I was merely trying to get a closer look at a shore bird seemed always, on both sides, a rather inadequate explanation.

But there were moments of great pleasure, too: the blue flash of a kingfisher over a still river, the sight of terns wheeling and diving into the sea, the tramp through fields and woods on sunlit days rewarded at the end by a glimpse of color or a burst of song. Many days and hours were happily filled in the pursuit of my hobby.

At Easter, one year, my father took us for a week's holiday in a valley in the south of Ireland, in Cork. We stayed at a small hotel. There were hills on either side of us, there was a lake, and in the lake was a small island with an old church, and at Easter the island was covered with rhododendrons. There were many birds to be seen in this valley, and, one evening, as I was coming back toward the hotel, I found the carcass of a young bird. I could not identify it with certainty, but I felt sure it was a young raven. If this was so, then I was convinced I had stumbled upon a piece of ornithological evidence that would be appreciated in higher circles. For the raven was, as far as I knew, a rather uncommon bird. So I picked up the corpse and brought it back to the hotel. There was a certain excitement as I came walking toward the entrance, and an elderly gentleman came forward to ask me what I had. There happened to be an old shoe box lying near the door, and I picked up the box and carefully began to pack the corpse into it. The old gentleman was intrigued and asked me what I was doing. I explained that I had found this corpse, that I thought it was that of a raven, and that I was going to send

it off to the Museum of Natural History for positive identification.

"Identification?" said the man. "Don't you know what
it is?"

"I'm not sure," I said, "but I think it's a young raven."

"A raven? Sure, that's just a common or garden crow."

"Strictly speaking," I said, "there is no such bird as a
crow."

At this point, we were joined by a very fat priest, who
had bloodshot eyes and a rich sense of fun. He was a man
who, when we all were gathered at our various tables for
dinner, would engage in conversation with one of his
friends at a neighboring table and would discuss loudly his
recent visit to Russia, what he had told Stalin, how he had
journeyed to Samarkand to inspect the sanitary arrangements there, and all of this in matter-of-fact tones. He
always achieved his purpose, because there were always
visitors who had come only for a meal. They were usually
English, and they would sit, silent and entranced, and obviously feeling a little guilty at eavesdropping on so fas-
cinating a conversation. The priest, when he joined us in
the lobby, asked what was going on.

The other man said, "This fellow says that, strictly
speaking, there's no such thing as a crow. Sure, dammit, I
been shooting them for twenty years."

"Well," I said, "there is a bird called a hooded crow,
which is black and white. There are also black birds: jackdaws, rooks, and ravens. When people use the term 'crow,'
they can mean any one of these three. Usually they mean
jackdaws."

"Well, that's damn queer," said the other man. "I've
been shooting them for twenty years, and I know they're
crows." At this point, he stalked off. The priest let out a
great roar of laughter.

Meanwhile, I had finished packing my corpse; I addressed the package and persuaded my father to give me the money for postage to Dublin. This was the last I heard of it. I have sometimes tried to imagine what the reaction was in Dublin one morning when a shoe box was opened and found to contain the rapidly decaying corpse of a bird; whether or not it was a raven, I still cannot tell for sure.

Later that year, I went to a meeting of bird-lovers in Dublin. The meeting was held in a parochial hall. The lighting was rather inadequate, and the heat more so. About forty people showed up, including a Jesuit and a retired major of the British army, both of whom were obviously experts in the field. Most of the others in attendance were elderly women who looked fit and vigorous, many of whom probably took cold baths each morning. There was a sprinkling of parsons who looked as though they came from country parishes where the population belonged to a different denomination. I was the only schoolboy there, and I felt distinctly out of place.

I have no recollection of the subject matter of the proceedings, but I do have a distinct memory of an old man, with white hair and a hearing aid, a stiff collar, black clothes, a black waistcoat across which there was a gold watch chain, who talked for some considerable time about warblers, I think. As the talk went on, I felt a great weight of depression settling over me. After that meeting, and from that time on, my enthusiasm waned rapidly. Other interests appeared, and the red notebook in which I recorded the passage of birds was consigned to a shelf, and it eventually disappeared from sight.

PART IV

KERRY

13

Granny and the Old Home

After Granny and Peadar moved to Dublin, I began to spend my holidays with my father's parents in Kerry, in a world completely different from the one I knew in Dublin. Their house stood at the foot of a hill—one of perhaps a dozen houses in a small village. It had two storeys. Downstairs was a long kitchen with a stone floor, at one side of which there was a large open fireplace, where a fire was always burning; in this fireplace, all the cooking was done during the day, and, around it, the whole family and visiting neighbors gathered at night.

There was a small room beside the kitchen, called the living room or the dining room, but it was rarely used. It had a table, a few plain chairs, two armchairs, and in the corner a big chest in which tablecloths and such were kept. There were a few pictures on the walls. The room had a fireplace: On the mantelpiece were some photographs—of my father when he got his degree, of various members of the family when they were married, of young grand-children, and so on. But, for the most part, the room was unoccupied, and I suspect that it was used only when a special guest was thought to need an armchair instead of one of the ordinary kitchen chairs.

The real living in the house was done in the kitchen. On one wall hung the clock. In the corner beside the window was a long wooden table on which the food was prepared and where meals were served, and nearby was one chair that my grandfather or my grandmother usually occupied at mealtime. Behind them was a wooden dresser where the dishes were kept, the cups hanging from hooks, and, in the bottom of it, such things as flour and salt were stored. On the window was a small lace curtain, and, in the corner, an oil lamp that was lighted at night. The fireplace itself was very spacious. It had an upright iron bar and an arm, which could be swung out and from which various hooks were slung. Until she was very old, my grandmother did all the cooking, and I can remember her kneading the dough to make currant bread. She would put it into a black pot, hang it on one of the hooks, sometimes putting hot turf on the lid of the pot, and swing it in over the fire to bake. There were various kinds of pots, including a great big one into which were put the potatoes.

In one corner of the fireplace was a hole in which my grandmother kept her snuff and her pipe, but she did not keep her tobacco pouch there. She always kept that on her person. The only time I remember her producing the pouch of tobacco and leaving it in view was when she was sitting by the fire and intended to stay there for a while. Then, she would sometimes stuff the pouch into the hole in the wall, but, at all other times, she carried it with her, though she never smoked outside the house. When she wanted to have a smoke, which was not too often—when she was older, she would like to have a leisurely session—she pulled out her pipe, filled it, and relaxed by the fire. The pipe was made of clay and was rather short-stemmed, and got to be progressively shorter. I do not know whether it was that she gripped it too hard in her teeth or what happened, but it certainly seemed to shrink as time went on. She would take a page out of a newspaper, roll it up, and stick it right into the center of the fire to light, and then she would apply it to the pipe. She would puff and puff, and meanwhile she would be talking, and one of my great worries as a child came of watching the shrinking newspaper until it reached the point where there was only a tiny fragment left gripped between her thumb and forefinger, with the flame still on it, and at the very last instant she would pop that into the pipe, too, so that I suppose she must have gotten a taste that combined tobacco and old newspaper. Then, she would sit back and puff away, taking long, slow drags, and contributing to whatever conversation was going on.

Sometimes, instead of smoking the pipe, she would take snuff, which she kept in a little can that had once contained Colman's mustard. The labels had all been torn off, but it was full to the top with snuff, and, from time to time, she would take some. My recollection of her snuff-taking is a bit vague, and I am not sure that she would sneeze. As far as I can recall, she would take just one pinch, one long sniff in each nostril, and that was all.

She would sit there in the corner, quite a massive woman; she was massive not because she was physically that way but because she wore so many garments. She had a great, abiding fear of catching cold, and, to forestall this danger, she wore layer after layer of clothing, so that she was really very bulky when she sat, with the bulk of skirts and underclothing. She was slightly taller than my grandfather, as I remember. Her eyes were either green or a mixture of blue and hazel. She had a very pale complexion, and the pallor was brought out by the black headdress or scarf she invariably wore, which she took off only when she combed her hair, and which was very white except for an occasional yellowish patch or tinge here and there. I suppose that, in her younger days, she must have had auburn hair. She had a nose that all her sons inherited, which, when you first looked at it, was almost a boxer's nose, spreading at the bridge as if it had been broken. It really dominated the face. She had a rather wide face with long cheeks. She had very long tapering fingers.

She swished as she moved around, one layer of clothes moving against another, and she seemed always to wear the same amount of clothing, summer and winter. On a fine summer day, she would regularly caution everybody who was prepared to listen—and there were very few who were, on this subject—against the cold and try to persuade them to wear jackets, overcoats, and so on. She invariably dressed in black, except for a canvas-gray apron she always wore. I do not remember that she had any jewelry. Inside the apron, and, I think, inside the first skirt, was a pocket, which I presume was *the* secret pocket, where all her treasures were kept—her rosary, her pouch of tobacco, and a few coins and medals.

She had thirteen children, of whom my father was the second. The men all went on to become teachers, and some of the woman taught for a while before they got married. Two of them emigrated to the United States in the early

1920's and settled in Hartford, where they prospered but then lost everything in the 1929 crash. The others scattered around Ireland.

Upstairs in the house, there were four rooms, with bare wooden walls and bare wooden floors. The beds were enormous, and there seemed to be compartments underneath, where valuables could be stored. Under my grandfather's bed were two suitcases, in one of which he kept old schoolbooks. The other contained clothes and other valuables. As a child, I lay in one of these big beds and looked up at the wooden rafters and listened to the wind. There was always a wind: There was a special wind that came in the winter; there was a breeze that came in the summer; there was a spring breeze that went with the high tides; and there was a wind that carried the rain.

The house, from the outside, was not very remarkable. It was of dressed stone, rising to a slate roof, with a chimney on either end. There was a small hint of a garden. Outside the kitchen door, which was really the main door of the house, was a small hedge of fuschia, and I remember, as a boy, picking the blossoms off the hedge and sucking the bottoms of them to draw out the honey. Once you passed beyond the fuschia, you came into a field, the first of the fields that belonged to my grandfather. When you stood at the door and looked down through the gap in the hedges to the fields, you could see a landscape that ended abruptly with the Atlantic.

One part of the sea where the Blasket Islands lay was cut off from view by a mountain that rose to a sharp point, but, otherwise, you could watch the stretch of the ocean to the bare horizon. When you looked over the nearer landscape, you could see, over to the right, a little oratory or small church that was built in the seventh century, made of loose gray stones and put together painstakingly without

mortar, the walls rising up and arching in toward one another until they met in a point. Farther to the left, but
obscured from view behind the mountain, there are prehistoric beehive huts, made also of gray stones without
mortar, and over two thousand years old. The Blasket Islands themselves are small, but they are rich with all kinds
of memories and experiences. They were inhabited until
twenty years ago, and it was between them and the mainland that some of the unfortunate ships of the Spanish
Armada tried to struggle. Some struggled in vain—hence
the legends of the Spanish gold lying at the bottom of the
sea around there and the stories of the Spaniards who came
ashore and were massacred. If you went around to the side
of the house, on some days, you could see Mount Brandon,
the second highest mountain in Ireland. It is a rugged
mountain, with streaked patches of bog along the sides, and
on top of it is an oratory to which pilgrims sometimes used
to climb, although nobody climbs there any more. Beneath
it is Saint Brendan's Bay, and Saint Brendan's Bay and
Mount Brandon are reminders of a medieval legend of an
Irish saint who reputedly sailed westward across the Atlantic and was the first to sight the New World. All around
my grandfather's house, in the poor soil and the stones and
the occasional high crosses, some of which are over a thousand years old, are reminders of a very long history.

14

Daddy Lovett

Why we called my grandfather Daddy Lovett instead of Daddy Luibhéid I do not know, for everyone in his neighborhood spoke Irish. He was perhaps six feet tall. He was very thin and very wiry, and he had piercing eyes. When I first knew him, he was getting into his seventies and had no teeth. His nose was hooked, and his long jaw curved up to meet it. He liked to chew tobacco, and he had two hats—a Sunday hat and a hat for the rest of the week. The Sunday hat was a brown hard hat with a crease on top, which he wore when he went to Mass or for any other important occasion. On Saturday nights, he would sit in one of the chairs in the kitchen, and his son Paddy would shave him. This was one of the pleasures of his old age, to have somebody else do that particular job for him. Then, Paddy would shave himself, and, the following morning, they would get dressed up and go to Mass. For the rest of the week, my grandfather rarely bothered to shave, so that, by about Friday, he had stubble, which he would finger occasionally as he pondered a question. He had an old jacket and woolen trousers. He wore enormous, thick hobnailed boots. When he left the house and went somewhere he almost always carried a stick with him, and the stick served various purposes: It served to drive cattle, to hit an occasional recalcitrant donkey, and also to point out to someone like myself features of the landscape. The hill behind the house was about eight hundred feet high, and he would send one of the dogs up to collect the sheep while we stood at the gate. When the dog reached the top of the hill, it would be just a black speck from where we stood, and it would begin to round up the sheep. My grandfather would point the stick and shout, "Go way out!" and the dog would gather the sheep and bring them in.

My grandfather did not speak much, but, when he did, his words were usually well chosen. In company, he liked to listen. He had a sardonic sense of humor. His harshest criticisms were directed not at the world outside but at his in-laws' family, and even those words were always humorous, deprecating, and compassionate. If any of his children complained of pains in the joints, a tendency to rheumatism, or any other failing, he would promptly disclaim all responsibility for those failings, insisting that they all came from the Daly side—his wife's side—of the family. When my father would complain of aching knees, my grandfather would grunt and say, "Ha! Daly knees."

I remember that, when I was a child, at night, particularly a winter's night, the oil lamp would be lit in the window, the fire would be glowing in the center of the wall at the corner of the kitchen, and the family would all kneel to say the rosary. My grandfather would take his boots off and kneel on a chair, and I remember the strange wiry shadow he cast as he responded to the prayers or led them.

When he went to Mass, he wore a brown hat, a brown pinstripe suit, and a brown coat. In fact, the formal clothing of all the men in that neighborhood was either brown or navy. He got the horse and cart, climbed in, and set off down a road that twisted on for perhaps four miles before it led into the small village of Ballyferriter. In that village were a church, a police station, a few guest houses, but almost every second door was the entrance to a bar, where, besides drinks' being served, groceries, a raincoat, ropes, a rake, and pretty much anything needed at home was sold.

The church in Ballyferriter is a small one, and my grandfather would arrive there with all the others from the neighboring houses and villages. They would come in and tie up their horses. The women would all enter and move to the front of the church, and the men would hang around outside for a last gossip or a last pull on a cigarette. When it was time to go in, the older the man, the greater the tendency for him to move up to the middle of the church. Over all of this presided two priests, a parish priest and a long-suffering curate.

The parish priest, when I first went to Ballyferriter, was known as Father Tom. He was very old. Indeed, he lived to be over ninety. At the Sunday Mass, he usually delivered a sermon that was light on profound theology and heavy with sarcastic comments on his parishioners and their way of life. In particular, I remember distinctly that, when the semiannual dues were supposed to come in, Father Tom had a habit of reading out the list of those who had contributed and, furthermore, of what they had contributed. In reading it out, he would, of course, also make his own appropriate comments. I recall that, during the reading of one such list, a person who had contributed five shillings was congratulated on having finally seen the light and come through with something he should have paid long ago.

Father Tom was a very practical man, and his practicality showed itself in various ways. One of his parishioners, for example, had, for something like fourteen or fifteen years, gone to Mass every Sunday and hidden himself behind a pillar, where there was no view of the altar; he said his prayers as devoutly as the next man, until the point was once raised with him that, because he had never seen the actual ceremonies, perhaps in all those years he had never actually attended Mass. He began to develop scruples about this and eventually took the problem to Father Tom, who disposed of it very simply and very effectively by asking him if the collection plate had reached him there. When the parishioner answered in the affirmative, the reply was, "Well, then, you've been to Mass."

After Mass, the younger men would almost invariably go into the local pub, where there would be a pint of stout, cigarettes, and some talk. Presumably, the ladies went off and talked among themselves until the men reappeared to take them home.

When my grandfather stood at the door of his house, we would often ask him what the weather was going to be. He would look at the sky and say in Irish (which was the language the people of that area used among themselves), "It will rain at midday" or "The weather will clear at three o'clock," and as sure as he said it, it would be so. This skill at predicting the weather was not something he learned as a farmer working a patch of very poor land. It was something that belonged to his earlier days, when his farm was so poor and his family so big that he had to take to the sea. By day he farmed; by night, from March until September, he went to sea to fish. He and his companions (usually two others) went out in small canvas boats called *naomhogai*. They are pointed at each end and consist of a rough wooden frame covered with canvas caulked with tar. Sometimes, as a child, I would stand at the top of the cliffs and look down. By that time, of course, my grandfather no longer had to fish, but I could see these little boats taking off from the shore for the Blasket Islands, for example, and then heading in the opposite direction. Eventually, the currents would take hold of them, and they would, finally, by a combination of rowing and drifting and heaving-to, make it to their destination. It is a terrible sea. Even on the calmest day, as you stand on the top of the cliffs and look out, it is a green heaving mass, and you can look down at the gannets below, as they dive in. They are a marvelous sight, as they wheel, drop down, suddenly close their wings, splashing in through the top of the water and trailing bubbles behind them, and then emerge moments later, each with a fish in its bill. For a tourist on land, it is a marvelous sight, but it was quite a different matter for men who had to live off the sea—men like my grandfather, who, because they were poor, set off from the shore (there was no harbor, just a place to pull up the boats) and fished night after night to supplement a debt-ridden existence. These men never learned to swim, because they believed that, if you once got into trouble, the thing to do was to end it quickly—to go down with no fuss and to cause no trouble to one's companions.

Disaster hit many of those small boats. Some of them went out and never returned. Some of them returned only because of the skill of their crews. My grandfather, for example, became a skilled seaman, but he was seasick regularly. The ocean was not his natural habitat, but he took to it and he learned its secrets. One night, when he and his companions were out at sea, a sudden fog descended, blocking them off completely. They could see nothing except through a tiny break above them, which was big enough for them to catch sight of a few stars, and my grandfather steered the boat toward the shore, using only the small glimpse of stars through the fog above him. When he had come close enough to the shore, he knew he was safe, because, even though the fog had finally closed over them and the stars were no longer visible, he would tell where he was by the way the sea broke on the base of the cliffs. He brought the boat back to safety, navigating surely by the sound of the waves breaking on the rocks.

If you stood as a tourist, or if you stood like me as a small boy on those cliffs above, and looked out on a fine day, even then you wondered how any man in a small boat held together by canvas could survive. You would see them going out sometimes, and a wave would come, and they would vanish from sight. You wondered if that was the end, and then, all of a sudden, there would appear at the crest of the wave the three men in their little boat—the oars moving, the men straining, the boat kept firm and straight and steady as they rowed on.

Sometimes, I stood there when the days were stormy and the sea was rough. Below, the rocks were pitted with caves gouged out by the battering tide, for the sea is a wild sea there. It turns fearsome shades, and it rolls and heaves, and, when it crashes on the cliffs, the spray will rise two hundred and three hundred feet. On this sea, my grandfather and his friends fished mostly for mackerel, and they brought their catch to Dingle, where they sold it at an open market. When they failed to dispose of what they had caught, they would take the fish home, salt-cure it, and keep it for sale during the coming spring, when demand would again be high.

Still, it was not enough. His children were growing up, and, to get by, he often had to go into debt. But those to whom he owed money did not press him, and he managed to survive, and his children were reared and set on their way.

15

Dingle

For ordinary groceries and immediate needs, my grandfather or Paddy could go either to Ballyferriter on Sunday
after Mass or to a small combination bar and grocery about
a mile from the house, run by a man called John Paul. For
items such as clothes, boots, or harnesses, it was necessary
to take a trip to Dingle, and that meant a full day's traveling. Dingle was about seven or eight miles away. One had
to go along a road that skirts the hill, rises, and then begins
to descend in a long, very straight run into Dingle. It is a
small town beside the bay. In my father's time, it was a
thriving community. It was there that he began teaching
when he was eighteen years of age, before he moved on to

Galway, where he met my mother. But, from the time I was old enough to go to see it, it was already very much in decline.

However, when my father or my grandfather went there, the trip was a major event. There was not just the practical problem of buying necessities but also the opportunity of visiting old friends and seeing the various relatives who ran stores or lived in the town. Much of what my grandfather bought was obtained in a store belonging for generations to a family called Curran, who had, in my grandfather's younger days, proved to be good, understanding friends, who gave him what he needed to keep his family going and were not too pressing about claiming payment of his debts to them. When I first got to know the store, it was presided over by a widow who was dressed solidly in black and wore glasses that had gray rims; she was kindly to everyone. There was a bar at one side of the store; at the other were shoes and waders and ropes— everything a man or woman could want. Blouses, dresses— all could be bought there, in the one room.

But this was not the only shop to be visited. There were several others along the way, into which my father would turn and in which he would meet friends, have a drink, and talk. It was in one such store that I first heard the tale of the virtues of Powers Gold Label Whiskey. This was the story of an elderly bachelor who lived alone in a small farmhouse and who came into one of these stores one day, choked with a cold. In the course of sympathizing with the man, the owner of the place suggested that he take home with him some Powers Gold Label to help relieve the cold. The man said he did not drink at all, but the barkeeper insisted he should take some home and try it. He told him to take a pint of Gold Label before going to bed and a second pint after getting in. A few weeks later, the man came into the store again and the barkeeper asked him if he had managed to cure the cold. The man said he had done as he was told. He had taken a pint of Gold Label before going to bed and remembered nothing more until he woke up the following morning lying stark naked on the stone floor, with the fire out and his cold gone.

The families who ran these stores and the customers who patronized them had long memories, and the tales they liked to repeat were frequently of events that were many years old. More than once, I heard the story of the French trawler that dropped anchor in Dingle harbor shortly after World War I. The captain came ashore, and, outside a bar, he was halted by the astonishing loveliness of a woman passing by. When he entered the bar, he began at once to tell the owner about the beautiful woman he had just seen, and he asked who she was and where she lived. There was another customer in the bar, and he was listening. Moving over beside the captain, he told him he knew the woman and he guaranteed that, for the sum of ten pounds, he would have her at the quayside at six o'clock, and he promised she would sail away to France with the captain. The captain eagerly paid the ten pounds; the two men shook hands; and the customer hurried off to find the woman, who, in fact, was his wife.

"Get your shopping done quickly, for we must be leaving early," he told her, and, by six o'clock, they were out of Dingle and back home. A few hours later the captain (who had been impatiently pacing the quay) reported the affair to the local barracks of the Royal Irish Constabulary, whose members found the story much too entertaining to require serious investigation. Thirty years later, the story was still discussed in the bars of Dingle, and the customer who had fooled the captain was known in all the neighborhood as the man who sold his wife.

In his earlier days, my grandfather occasionally went as far as Tralee, which is thirty miles away. He would go to a cattle fair, bringing some cows to sell and hoping to buy others. Getting there meant walking, driving the cattle before him. When nightfall came, he stopped in one of the houses along the way, where he was taken in and fed and where there would be talk and exchange of news. The following morning, he went on his way again. That trip, which we often made by car, was a delightful one. But, for a man who had to walk it, it must have been rather different, for the roads are long and steep. There was a train there, too, the line running beside the road, but, of course, my grandfather could not take his cows on the train.

The Dingle Railway has long since vanished, but it must have been marvelous fun while it was there. The train set off from Tralee, and, midway on the journey, at a place called Annascaul, it would stop and everybody would get out and have a drink, including the driver, and they would gather together. Then, when everybody was ready—nobody was rushed—the train would resume its trip. Every journey had its fondly remembered incidents. Women went into Tralee to do their shopping. One woman had bought a bucket, and, because her feet were tired by the end of the day, she sat on the bucket on the platform, waiting for the train to come in. One of the local newsboys came up to her and asked, "Paper, Missus?" to which she replied, "Go 'way out o' that, ye dirty divil, I'm only sittin' on it."

There were first- and third-class carriages on this train, though what the difference was is hard to imagine. Once, when a group of women who had done a day's shopping in Tralee found themselves, with their articles and their boxes and their bales, unable to get a seat in a third-class car, they went into the first-class section. When the ticket collector, who was new to the line, tried to get first-class tickets from them, the women all banded together, took his trousers off, threw them out the window, and then told him that, if they were not left alone, something worse might happen to him. So he withdrew.

The old cry "Cow on the line!" was very common on those trips. Regularly, the train would be stopped while the driver or some of the passengers got out to clear away some stray cattle or goats or sheep or whatever had wandered into the way.

Still, for my grandfather, going to the fair in Tralee, there was no question of taking the train. He had to walk there, and he had to walk back. He walked along through various small towns. In one of them was the South Pole Inn, opened and owned by one of the men who had previously joined Scott on his expedition to the Antarctic.

16

Things Cultural

As time went on, I began to notice something about my grandfather and his neighbors that increasingly astonished me. Here were people often in wretched circumstances, their land poor and the burden of debt frequently on them; and yet, for all the hardness of the conditions in which they had to live, they had an extraordinary preoccupation with language. I observed that one of the greatest compliments that could be paid to a person was to say that he or she spoke well. I came slowly to realize that, in the Irish they spoke, there was a richness, a variety, a poetic concern that bore no relationship to the material circumstances of their lives and that, as far as I could gather, seemed to have been a preoccupation of generations before them.

My great-grandmother could neither read nor write, and still she was able to recite the complete works of Seán Clárach MacDomhnaill, one of the more classical figures in Irish poetry. When asked how she had come to acquire this extensive lore of poetry, she answered that, as a child, she had listened to a visitor in her house reciting the entire work, and, on the basis of having heard it once, she was able to preserve it in her memory until she was an old woman. When my father asked her how it was possible to remember so much after hearing it only once, her reply was that, among her friends, it would be considered a disgrace not to be able to pick up a large quantity of poetry on first hearing, and it was their custom after a recitation to go through what had been recited together, so that any part that was missed by one member of the audience could be picked up from some other member who had heard it and remembered it.

Her husband, my great-grandfather, had shared this pre-occupation with poetry, but he had added to it a wide interest in world affairs, such as they were known. He could read, and he read avidly any papers that came his way. One day, when he was an old man, he announced that he would die the following day. He took to his bed, and the members of his family tried to make fun of his prediction. But, somehow, the authoritative way in which he had made the announcement compelled a reluctant belief that perhaps he might be right. Some neighbors came to visit him, and one of them arrived with a newspaper. The old man asked if he had read the paper. The neighbor replied that he had. The old man then asked for a full account of what was in the paper and particularly of what was being debated in Parliament. At this, my great-grandmother remonstrated with him:

"Isn't it making your peace with God you should be

now, when you are going to die, instead of bothering with that nonsense about Parliament and newspapers and the like?"

"I have made my peace with God," he said, "and there is nothing more to be said on that score. But when I get in tomorrow, they'll all be wanting to know the news, and I'll want to be having the latest for them."

The following day he was dead, as he had predicted.

This interest in language was something that my grandfather inherited from him. When my father was busy at the task of translating one of the plays of W. B. Yeats for the Abbey Theater, he brought the text with him to Kerry, and, at one or two points where he could find no Irish that would do justice to the original poetry, he asked my grandfather for help. At every point where my father was at a loss, my grandfather was able to supply a felicitous translation. His neighbors would have expected him to be able to give that help, just as he, in turn, felt a certain obligation to be able to do so.

So, the talk was frequently not only of the doings of neighbors but also of what they had said and the way they had said it, and treasured sayings were repeated over and over again and passed from house to house. This preoccupation with language was to yield much fruit. Perhaps the most startling was to be found on the Blasket Islands. If you stood on the cliffs and looked out over the heaving ocean to the craggy, sea-whipped rocks that lay off the tip of the land, if you looked at the biggest island, where, in the shadow of a hump of scraggy pasture, a few small abandoned houses huddled together, it was hard to realize that two of the great classic works of modern Irish literature were written here, and written not by visiting authors but by an old woman and an old fisherman who had lived out long years on those rocks, where the spray rose high

and the Atlantic winds roared. One of them was Tomás
Ó Criomhthain, whose book *An tOileánach* (*The Island
Man*) is regarded by all who speak Irish knowledgeably
as one of the great works of modern Ireland. This man was
poor. He came off the island to the mainland perhaps half
a dozen times in his life, and, yet, his book is an astonish-
ingly rich portrayal of island life, in a language of endless
poetry and remarkable subtlety. When he wrote it, he had
probably seen no more than five or six books in the course
of his long lifetime.

The other book was *Peig*, written by Peg Sayers, an
autobiography, and it, too, is powerfully written. This
remarkable concern with language and poetry was summed
up for me when, as a teenager, I went into Dingle Hospital
one day with my father to visit my grandmother. The
women's ward was a long plain room with plain floor
boards and iron-framed beds. In a bed in one corner was
Peg Sayers. She was old and blind, but there was a remarkable beauty about her face. I was brought over and introduced to her, and we talked briefly; at the end, the
compliment she paid my father was to say that I spoke
Irish well. It was clear from the attitude of the women
around me, the wives of farmers and fishermen, that I was
considered to have been very greatly honored by this com-
plimentary remark of Peg Sayers.

17

Christmas and Other Holidays

I spent many holidays in Kerry as a child. Christmas in particular was a magical time. On Christmas eve, I would look out the window, and, at that time (this was in the early 1940's), there was no electricity at all in that area. So, you would look out, and at first there would be almost total blackness, the blackness of the land, which would shade into the near blackness of the sea and the sky beyond. Then, as it came toward nine and ten o'clock, when it would soon be time to go to Mass, you would see pinpoints of candlelight all over the landscape. In every window of every house a candle burned, and in every house the preparations were going on for the trip to the church for midnight Mass. In my grandfather's house, we all got ready and out of the house almost an hour before Mass was due to begin. A horse and cart were waiting, and in the cart was a pile of straw. We had our coats on and were all bundled up, and we set off down the hard, bumpy road toward Ballyferriter and the church. As we went along the main road, other families came out of the side roads bound in the same direction. There would be a shout of greeting, and you would hear the echo of the iron rims of the wheels of the cart behind you as they bounced along.

When we got to the church, in one corner was an old organ, and there were a few girls who sang hymns. There were Mass and a sermon and mutual greetings, and then out again and another delay, while everyone greeted everyone else, and then back into the cart and on back to the house. I remember vividly lying on my back, warm, with a thick coat on and my head covered and a load of straw around me to keep the wind off, my grandfather sitting up in front, holding the reins, his legs dangling over the side and the cart bouncing along. I lay on my back and looked up at a sky that was completely free of clouds. Millions of stars were out that first Christmas I spent in Kerry. When we arrived at the house, at nearly two o'clock, a goose had been cooked, and there were cakes, tea, and drinks. When I had had something to eat, I was sent off to bed, while the older people—including my father and my grandfather—sat around the fire and talked, and the hum of their talk was the last thing I could hear in my bed. I could hear it through the wooden floorboards, on which there was no carpet. Outside, a light wind blew in off the sea.

I spent many nights like this in Kerry—when I lay awake in bed, and there was only a dim light, and I could hear the wind that came in off the Atlantic. It could be heard in the rafters and all around the house. But, inside, the house was warm and snug.

Kerry also meant the day after Christmas, Saint Stephen's Day, when the Wren Boys came. It was a custom in Kerry, as in other rural areas of Ireland, that, on that day, the young people captured a wren, put it in a cage, dressed up in costume, and, carrying the wren, went from house to house to sing and dance and be given gifts, sometimes money but more often sweets and other good things to eat. The custom is still preserved in some parts of Ireland but not to the extent that I knew it in the early years of the war. At that time, large groups of young people would dress up, and many of them were musicians; many of them could play the tin whistle or the melodian; some of them, even a violin. They would come into the kitchen of my grandfather's house and sing and dance, and, for a few moments there would be a great burst of revelry and laughter and applause, and then they would move on to the next house. We would wait until another group would arrive. And so it would go throughout most of the morning and most of that day.

I spent summers too in Kerry. The fields had turned greener and along the roads were great solid masses of fuschia and yellow gorse, and there were birds—yellowhammers and cuckoos and many others. There were the long summer nights—at that time of the year it was still daylight until 11:30 at night. The sun would begin to sink into the Atlantic, and, long after it had gone below, there would still be a certain amount of light. Sometimes at 10:00 at night, or even later, perhaps, there would be just a certain lessening of the light, but you could still see everything clearly. In the summer, there was much to do around the farm, driving the horses or exploring the fields. Several fields away from the house was a stream, where I went often. The water was ice cold, and it was fun to spend hours there, diverting the course of the stream, moving stones here, there, and around.

It was during one of those early summers that I caught pneumonia. I was working on the side of a hill with a cousin. We were playing at being grown-up men cutting turf, and I cut a few sods in my clumsy fashion, and I remember feeling a strange tightness or rawness in the throat and beginning to perspire. That night I was put to bed, and the local nurse was sent for to come and have a look at me. Her name was Nurse Rabbit. She had gray hair and wore a navy blue uniform. She rode on a bicycle from house to house in the district under her charge. She came in and took my temperature, and she smiled through her rather thick-lensed glasses, and I heard her talking to my grandmother in the kitchen below: "He's very bad. You'll have to send for the doctor at once. I'm nearly sure it's pneumonia."

I seem to have lost a sense of time and of the way things moved in the days that immediately followed. A doctor came and prescribed tablets with the mysterious letters *M* and *B*. I remember coming to at one stage during the night, lying in my bed, and seeing a shadow over in the corner of the room. It was my grandmother. I did not know then that she had spent the entire night in the rocking chair beside me as I went through the crisis of the illness.

That was during the war. I was alone in Kerry. My father and mother had sent me there and gone on a cycling holiday through County Wicklow on the east coast. Now the question was to try to get through to them word that I was ill. It took a great deal of trouble, but they were finally located. I vaguely remember hearing that my father was coming, and I remember lying in bed suffering all sorts of discomforts and having to drink several horrid liquids.

There was a mixture half of hot water and half of milk, the taste of which still lingers with me twenty-five years later, a nasty concoction I had to take every hour. I remember, too, lying in a bed from which the sheets had been removed lest I catch cold, wrapped in blankets, sweating profusely, and not allowed to put a finger outside, in case my pneumonia got worse.

The only hope on the horizon was the thought that my father was coming. They kept assuring me he was on his way, and eventually he did come. He managed to come on one of those train trips that, during the war, took many long hours; so, when he finally reached the house, he was utterly exhausted. I was asleep when he arrived. When I awoke in the morning, there was a bed at the foot of my own and he was in it. I called to him repeatedly, and finally he sat up. He was so tired that one eye remained shut and the other one half-opened. He looked at me, and I said, "Daddy, I don't want to have to drink that mixture of milk and water ever again." He said, "All right, you won't have to." He fell back and, within seconds, was snoring. I lay back in my bed, completely content. The worst was over. I would not have to drink that concoction any more, and my father was there.

In the days before he came, I lay in the enormous bed with a terrible boredom settled on me. Finally, the only thing I could do was to dream myself out of where I was, into a huge railway yard right in the center of Ireland, from which trains ran every five minutes to Dublin and Cork and Galway and north to Belfast, stopping everywhere along the way. In the middle of this vast yard was only one signalman, myself. All the responsibility of keeping all the trains running fell on me. Hour after hour, I manipulated imaginary signals, I switched tracks, I redirected trains. Express trains crossed Ireland with a speed that was absolutely unknown in the real world, where travelers moved from one station to the next and wondered if there would be enough fuel to last until the train reached its destination. For two, perhaps three, days, this was how I lived, until my father finally came.

If the memories of those early holidays in Kerry are vivid for me, the excitement of them was nothing compared to what it must have been in my father's day, when a vast community of young men and young families lived there together before emigrating to Dublin, Cork, Britain, the United States, Canada, or even farther away. I could see, in more recent years, when my father went to Kerry, that it was not at all the place he had known. He used to tell me of the nights spent in a certain house where an entire village would gather to hear the stories of men who had traveled beyond Dingle and Tralee and who carried with them the lore of the areas in which they had journeyed. An honored place would be kept for them, and a whole village would be enthralled by the stories they had to tell. Or there were the young men who used to play tricks on one another, who dressed up as ghosts and scared the superstitious, or who ran and gamboled and played in the fields and on the farms round about.

There was another house my father used to tell about—a house not too far away from his own—whose members were distinguished for their absolute terror of ghosts and such. Naturally, the house became the center for all kinds of ghostly activity, dreamed up and performed by neighboring children and young men. The house was visited one night by a young neighbor who crept around and was able to put his hand inside a window and make the shade fall, so that the members of the household were startled, and all sorts of things happened around the house, until, eventually, in a panic, two women ran upstairs, jumped into the bed where their old grandfather was lying, and refused to get out for fear of the ghosts. The old grandfather, lying peacefully and smoking his pipe, was finally compelled to get up and find a pitchfork. He knew perfectly well who the ghost was. And he often said afterward that it was a good thing he never caught his quarry, because the ghost would certainly have had a pitchfork in his backside by which to remember that night.

But, when I first went there for my holidays, as a young boy, all this was over, and most of the houses were occupied by aging men with whom perhaps one or two younger sons had remained, and the others had scattered throughout the world. But, for all that, it was in many ways a gay place. For a young boy like me, coming from Dublin, a visit to Kerry and all the fun associated with it not only lived on in the weeks following such a holiday but still live on with a certain sparkle and a certain gaiety.

18

Daddy Lovett's Last Days

My grandfather spent his life in that region. Tralee was the farthest away he would normally go. If he traveled to Dublin or Galway or some such place, it was usually for a special event such as the wedding of a son or a daughter. After a week in Dublin, he was more than happy to get back to his own house, his farm, his friends, his church, and his view of the sea. He looked forward keenly to the visits of his sons and daughters, who lived all over Ireland and who all tried to come to the old home regularly. Whenever his sons came to visit him, they invariably brought him some whiskey, and he kept the bottle in the bed. A bottle lasted him many weeks, for he took just a mouthful now and again at night. He lived for these visits, and, when they came, there was gaiety in the way he walked and in the way he listened. The sardonic front he usually presented to the world tended to crumble. Sometimes, he could not repress the joy in him. On one occasion, one of my father's brothers took him for a drive in the car, and they went around by the cliffs over the sea, and my grandfather could restrain himself no longer—he burst into song. He sang songs of his youth and songs he had learned as a child, many of which had been old before he was born.

But there was little gaiety in the last weeks of his life. Paddy, his youngest son, who had stayed at home to help on the farm and who had in fact taken over the running of it, was found seriously injured beside his bicycle, and the news reached us late one night in Dublin. My father and I set off in the small hours of the morning and drove through the darkness. Near Limerick, we ran into heavy fog. I was driving, and all I could do was turn the lights onto the grass margin of the road, steer by that, and hope for the best. Suddenly, an enormous whiskey bottle fifteen feet high loomed in front of us. We got out to investigate and discovered that I had followed the margin into a garage, had passed the pumps, which I had not seen at all, and had come up against a billboard shaped to represent a bottle of whiskey. We found the road again and pushed on, until finally we reached Tralee and the hospital where Paddy lay. He was unconscious, and it was clear that only a few hours of life remained for him. We left him and drove on to my grandfather's house.

It was early afternoon; the sun was high; there was a blue sky; it was May. There was birdsong around us. All the men were standing outside the house. The women were inside. Up the long road came a little red Fiat. It pulled up, and a guard got out. He spoke to my father. The news had come that Paddy was dead. My father had to tell my grandfather, who was standing outside, holding his old walking stick. My father simply said to him that Paddy had gone. The old man gripped his stick, looked down, and said, "Oh, my. Oh, my." That was all he said, but the way he said it reflected all the anguish and loss that he had known in his long life.

He went back to working the farm, and, for the next month, he tried to work as he had been able to do thirty years previously. Then, one day, as he came out of a shed, he slipped, fell, and broke his hip. Forty-eight hours later he was dead. With his death, there ended, at least for me, the special quality of pleasure that had been associated with Kerry and with holidays there.

My grandmother remained in Kerry for a few years but eventually moved to Dublin, where she lived out her last years with one of my aunts.

Paddy's widow and children continued to live in the old home. Every spring, the neighbors gathered to plant her fields for her, and, in the long autumn, they reaped the crops for her, until her children were reared and her need was past.

PART V

SECONDARY-SCHOOL YEARS

19

Belvedere: The First Four Years

"So you'll be going to secondary school in September?" asked the mother of a former desk mate.

"Yes," I said.

"And will you like that?" she asked.

"I don't know," I said.

"And where are you going to go?" she asked.

"To Belvedere," I said.

"Oh. Belvedere." And the tone, the slight raising of her voice, gave me the obscure feeling that I had somehow offended her. Her boy had already begun to earn a living in a grocery store. In the way she pronounced the name Belvedere, I caught an echo of an attitude I had encountered before and would meet again, a resentful suspicion that Belvedere was not the place for the sons of ordinary mortals, that its playground echoed only to the shouts of young aristocrats. I was very puzzled by it all, and I waited with some interest to become a part of these new surroundings.

I had been enrolled in the school one summer morning. My father and I got off the bus under the pointed Gothic spire of Findlater's Church, and we turned into Denmark Street, walking along past the Georgian houses on our left. This line of houses was broken roughly in the middle, where one house detached itself from the row on either side. We went up its flight of steps and were shown to a waiting room, which had a parquet floor with no carpet, a big table, and, set between two high windows, a bookcase. The bookcase contained volumes by former Belvederians, and I noticed with some interest even then that, although the spiritual writings of Dom Columba Marmiom and the economic theories of a famous professor were to be found there on the shelves, there was one significant omission: Not one of the books by James Joyce was in sight.

The rector appeared; we all shook hands; and then I was a silent witness to the proceedings of the next twenty minutes or so, during which my father outlined the work I had done in primary school and gave some information about my educational background. When the talk was done, it was conveyed to me that I was an acceptable candidate for admission to the school. From the tall windows, the sunlight fell across the rector. He smiled at me; we shook hands; and it remained to await the coming of September, when the leaves would begin to turn and the gates of the school would open.

When I went to Belvedere, it was not my first contact with the Jesuits. I had met several of them in Peadar's house in Galway, and, for many years, one Jesuit came every

Friday afternoon to visit the house in Dublin. He used to arrive at six o'clock, signaling his presence in an unmistakable way by raising the door knocker to its highest point and letting go, so that the bang reverberating through the house was sufficient to let us know who had arrived. He left his bicycle outside the door or, sometimes, wheeled it onto the porch. He would sit by the fire and eat a boiled egg, two slices of toast, and two cups of cocoa. In the ten or so years I watched him at this, he would occasionally vary this routine to the extent of having a fried egg instead of a boiled one, and, when he did, he consumed the white of the egg first and then slowly, delicately eased the tip of his knife under the yolk, raised it gently, held it suspended for a moment over his dish, and then swallowed it whole. Then he sat back and talked about what seemed to be a predetermined schedule of topics: a weighty theme invariably followed by a lighter one. Once or twice, because he was a professor of moral theology, I put a question to him, and, on such occasions, he would draw himself up in his chair as though mildly insulted and put his fingertips together; as soon as I saw these preparations, I felt an instantaneous regret that I had bothered to open my mouth. He acquired a solemnity that to me was a sad thing to behold. But he was kindly, and we all liked him. He had a passion for soccer, and, each week, he went to whatever match was in progress, and he would report to us, kick by kick, what had happened.

The one thing he did not prepare me for before I entered the gates of Belvedere was the winged soutane worn by the Jesuits in their house or at school. I presumed then, as I do now, that the two lengths of black cloth hanging from the shoulders of the soutane had some liturgical significance. If so, the wearers seemed to have forgotten the fact, and these wings were used to dust chairs, to remove chalk from boards, to provide arm rests, and so on.

The classrooms were designed to accommodate about twenty-five students, and they were titled in a way that seemed completely mysterious to me. A fifth-year student claimed to be in "Poetry"; a sixth-year student, in "Rhetoric." Within each year group, divisions were made according to educational background and talent, and, when I started, there were four groups in first year, the curriculum being graded accordingly.

We sat at our desks and did our work, and, when someone stepped out of line, varied punishments were available. The usual system was for the transgressor to be called to the desk of the person conducting the class to receive a note stating what the misdemeanor was. He took the note downstairs and joined a line outside the office of the Prefect of Studies. In this line, there were usually half a dozen students from various classes, and we all stood around and looked as if we were discussing the weather and pretended not to notice the pitying glances of our fellow students as they passed by safe and unscathed. One by one we walked into the office of the Prefect of Studies; he read the note, took out a little stamp bearing his signature, and affixed his name to the note. He then handed the note back to us and produced a strap, which descended with greater or lesser severity on outstretched hands. We then returned to class and gave the note back to the teacher.

There was also a system of detention. One could be kept after school to do work, which was supervised by some scholastic who had been assigned duty for that week. If one failed to await detention, there was a call the following morning from the Prefect of Discipline. One could see the black shadow looming outside the frosted glass of the door. There would be a knock; someone would open the door;

the name of the unfortunate student would be called out. He would walk outside, and we would all listen to hear the slap of leather on hands. He would reappear with a look on his face suggesting an anxiety to reach his desk before his hands fell off.

But there was nothing brutal or humiliating about this system of punishment, and we understood this very well as we listened to stories of what happened in some other schools in the city. We noticed, too, that stupidity was never a crime and that, however much exasperation it might provoke in this or that teacher, the student in question was never led to believe that he was somehow an inferior being.

I ate lunch in the refectory during the first few years. We all marched in and took our places at a row of tables. We stood and waited for the Father Minister to come in to say grace, and, after he had done so, we sat down. The system was inevitably weighted in favor of the older boys, who came in first and took the places nearest the serving tables, which meant that they often got the food when it was warm. By the time it reached the ends of the tables where the junior students sat, the food was often cold; it was usually quite awful anyway. It was not much consolation to remember that the Jesuits who lived in the house had to eat the same stuff. I tried one day to improve my lot by dashing in and taking a place at one of the tables where the senior boys congregated. I was not there long when a tall sixth-year student came and told me to get going, that that was his place. I argued with him that we all sat on a first-come, first-served basis. This argument, reasonable as it seemed to me, made no headway with him at all. He grabbed me by the back of the neck and the seat of the trousers and began to haul me away. I gripped the table, and, as he pulled me, the table also moved, with a great clatter of knives, forks, glasses, and jugs. This drew the attention of the Father Minister, and my tormenter, seeing this, had to let go. He uttered a number of dire threats, but I still held on. Then he told me that, if he ever caught me there again, I would suffer a "dig in the snitch," which I assumed to mean a poke in the nose, though I am not quite sure. My persistence was rewarded, however, by warm food and a slice of quite good meat that day. But, by the next day, preparations had been made to forestall any attempt to usurp the places of the mighty; the senior boys were there before me, and they all gave me a menacing look as I came in. So I moved farther down, to my old place.

The Father Minister was a mild man, and, when we got out of hand, as we sometimes did, he would give us a pained, sorrowful look. Of course, he had one ultimate weapon that he could use, though he never did, and that was to order the removal of all the food if we did not behave. Such a catastrophe was something we all strove to avoid.

My first two years in Belvedere were academically disastrous. The little work I did was undertaken strictly to keep out of trouble. For the most part, I was deeply bored. I learned poems such as "Young Lochinvar" and "The Lady of Shalott" and pulled them apart to find assonance and alliteration, metaphor and simile. We read *Alice in Wonderland*, which struck me then as a children's book written by a grown-up for other grown-ups. We began a survey of European history, starting with the barbarian invasions and ending with the reign of Louis XIV. It was all a list of dates and battles and names, which we committed to memory. We started to learn French, which was fun, and we read geography, which was not. We had an unbelievably dull textbook that listed all the rivers in Ireland and told us about industry and agriculture, dairy farming, and the like, and from there we moved on to surveys of what was produced in Bristol and whether or not the Mediterranean had tides. We learned Latin and read Irish; we did mathematics and began a long, six-year course in Christian doctrine. The green report slips came back to my father at Christmas, at Easter, and in the summer, and the tale they told was always the same—that I was at the bottom of the class, that my marks were among the lowest of my group, and that I had better get a move on if I was to survive.

In my second year, we were transferred to a different classroom, and I could look over rooftops to the spire of Saint George's Church. I found a desk at the back of the room, which offered several advantages. It had a hole at one side, which enabled me to slip clandestine books into it and to read them undisturbed by whichever teacher was conducting the class session. I also found it convenient as a place to work on a class newspaper, which I produced at intervals of about ten days. Much of my time was spent gathering material. I stole jokes wherever I could find them, and I ran a page that seemingly was popular—an astrological column, which foretold each week the disasters that would befall the various members of the class. Because I could not draw, the paper was weak on cartoons, but I made up for it with collages and some jokes that I hoped would remedy whatever deficiency struck the eye. I also ran a contest in which names were scrambled and the winner got a packet of fruit pastilles with the compliments of the newspaper. All of this seemed much more satisfactory to me than the scholastic scheme of things, for, by then, I had been introduced to the study of Greek, we were taking a long look at the guild system of the Middle Ages, and I was enveloped in an ever deepening fog when the topic at hand was mathematics. We also spent one hour a week in an art room, where we were expected to master the elements of drawing. In this, I was a complete failure, and a tacit agreement existed between the teacher and my-self, to the effect that, if I kept quiet and stayed out of trouble, he would not bother me. As a result, the main recollection I have of drawing class is of an afternoon when one of my fellow students, the son of a well-known Labor leader, threw down his pencil, stood up, and delivered a speech on the theme that the workers of Ireland are the backbone of the people. We all listened without comment; the teacher drew a few more ellipses; and work was re-sumed.

We were taught English literature by a scholastic named Veale, and we did terrible things to his name. We read some of the prescribed authors, wrote essays, and learned poems. But, every Wednesday, Mr. Veale provided us with what we quickly came to recognize as a treat. Wednesday was our so-called half-day, which meant that we were allowed to go home one hour earlier than usual, but we had to compensate for this lost hour by staying on Saturday morn-ing until dinnertime. Every Wednesday, Mr. Veale came in and made himself comfortable at the rostrum. Then, he would produce a book and begin to read to us for an hour —essays, poems, sections of novels and plays. Each week, there was something new, and I was introduced to many authors of whom I had previously been ignorant. These sessions earned us no marks, and there were no questions about them in the examination; yet, for me, they were the high points of the year. For what Mr. Veale conveyed most of all in the pieces he chose and in the way he read them was that literature need not be a stuffy exercise, that it could have a vibrant life of its own.

Another new face in my second year was that of our teacher of Latin, a Jesuit named Father Nolan, who wore glasses and whose hair was silver and wavy and swept straight back. What I noticed particularly about him, the first day I met him, was a certain elegance of language, a certain felicity of usage, which left me a bit uneasy. I had the feeling that somewhere a devastating epigram was waiting to be launched. But I need not have worried, for, within a matter of days, I came to realize that Father Nolan was one of the most patient and gentle individuals I had ever encountered. He opened many worlds to me when I was a boy, and, twenty years later, I think of my relationship with him as one of the best friendships I ever made.

So the weeks rolled by; the work was there to be done; and I did as little as I could. I had one bad moment, around the middle of November, when we were summoned to an audition in the school gymnasium. Each year one of the Gilbert and Sullivan operettas was put on at Christmas, and I was called, as were other members of my class, for a voice test. I had an all-consuming fear that I might be picked; so, when the moment came, I produced as unmusical a croak as I could manage, with the result that I was not invited even to join the chorus.

Easter came and then the summer, and, when the report of the examination was delivered to the house in June, it showed that, out of a class of twenty-five, I had managed to achieve nineteenth place. The comment of the Prefect of Studies was that the time had come to take a very serious appraisal of what I was going to do. Cold winds, indeed, were beginning to blow. The two public examinations on which a future career could depend, one of which was at the end of my third year, were hovering in sight, and I knew that my situation was in drastic need of improvement.

So, in my third year, I began to work, not because I wanted to but because I realized I had no choice. My resolve was helped by the fact that some of the curriculum was getting more interesting. Instead of studying the Greek alphabet, we were now reading a Greek play. Instead of writing simple French sentences, we were beginning to read French novels. We were reading English drama. In addition to all this, we took what I now suppose was a relic of a long-dead past—a gentleman's course in science. Once a week, we went down to the physics and chemistry lab and sat on tall stools around tables. Our teacher was well aware of the fact that we knew nothing about the subject, so he became a kind of magician, playing tricks with Bunsen burners and beakers, turning fluids various colors, causing containers to collapse, shunting mercury with a spoon.

"And you know what Lloyd George said about de Valera when they were negotiating the Treaty in 1921?" he asked.

"No!" we said.

"He said that dealing with de Valera was like picking up mercury with a fork." And he produced a fork and tried to pick up some mercury that was at hand. We were deeply impressed, and, for a moment, we left the world of science and contemplated the workings of diplomacy.

The curriculum began to get heavier, and our days at school had to be followed by many hours of study at night. My marks began to improve, until I discovered at last, and with some astonishment, that I was considered one of the surer candidates for honors at the public examinations.

20

France

In the middle of my fourth year, it was announced that a group of about twenty students from the school would be sent to France during the following summer, to live in the homes of French families, and parents were invited to consider whether they had the will and, more important, the money to send a son on this expedition. Despite the financial burden involved, my parents were highly enthusiastic that such an opportunity could come my way. My mother had been a student in France, and my father, being a teacher, well understood the value of such a trip. My name was, therefore, put in early as a prospective member of the expedition. As the year wore on, the final arrangements came to be made, and we learned that the families with whom we were to live had already been picked. All that remained was to await the day of departure, and I did so with the greatest possible impatience.

We flew from Dublin airport one summer morning in one of the old DC-3's belonging to Aer Lingus. The flight took over three and a half hours, and we reached Le Bourget airport in Paris around lunchtime. It was warm when we landed, but the sky was gray. We boarded a bus and drove through the grim working-class area adjacent to the airport. The walls were covered with slogans, the most common protesting the fact that Jacques Duclos, a leader of the French Communist Party, was currently in prison: "*Libérez Jacques Duclos.*" There was the usual sprinkling of graffiti, including the usual denunciations of the United States. The houses seemed uniformly gray, and the paint was peeling from window frames and doors. But the bus drove on, and eventually a central cluster of buildings came into sight, which meant we were nearing the middle of the city. The bus pulled into the Gare des Invalides, where we were met by a Jesuit, who brought us into a room and assigned each of us to a member of the family with whom he would be living.

I was introduced to Jacques, a tall, swarthy boy, whose black hair was cropped short and who had enormous feet, which seemed too big even for the pair of huge sandals he wore. He took one of my bags, and we set off. He led me across the Place de la Concorde and up the Champs Elysées until we came within a few hundred yards of the Arc de Triomphe. Then, he turned down a side street, and I followed him obediently until we came to an apartment house. We got into an elevator; Jacques produced a small coin, which he put into a slot; the elevator quivered and shook; and we rose at length to the fifth floor. We emerged onto a darkened landing and stood an instant, listening to the clatter of the elevator as it descended, empty, to the ground floor. Jacques then beckoned me to follow, and we entered a comfortable apartment belonging to a family that, I was to discover as time went on, was wealthy but believed in the virtues of frugal living. Four other children and the parents appeared to greet me. They did so politely and with some curiosity and also, I felt, with some disappointment, as though I had shattered a cherished picture of what Irishmen looked like. I was given a room and told that, on the following day, we would all leave Paris for Brittany, where the family had rented a house and where I would pass some of the coming weeks. All this was conveyed to me in rapid-fire Parisian French to which I only gradually adjusted. I was invited to withdraw to my bed to recover from the rigors of the trip I had undertaken that morning; I agreed to this and shut the door behind me. I lay on the bed, took my shoes and socks off, put my hands under my head, contemplated my toes, and listened to the noise of the traffic outside.

Next day, when we gathered for lunch, we were joined by an uncle who was the last of a vanishing species in France: He owned a chain of private banks. He was paunchy, had blond hair cropped short, and ignored all of us and spoke only to his brother-in-law, the man of the house. They talked of financial matters, while the rest of us ate in silence. When they had apparently finished, he leaned across, kissed his sister—first on the right cheek, then on the left, then on the right again—added a concluding sentence to what he had been saying to his brother-in-law, turned around, and disappeared. Then, there was a flurry of activity: Bags were packed; drawers were opened and shut; the maid hurried about; and, by six o'clock, everything was ready. Cars came to pick us up and brought us to the station. We boarded a train, and, at seven-thirty, we pulled out of the station and headed northwest.

We traveled all night, and I sat in my corner, dozing and then waking up suddenly and dozing again. We stopped many times. When dawn came, we halted at a station, and, as I looked out, I caught sight of two elderly women in black dresses, walking together. On their heads, they wore high stiff lace hats over which plastic covers had been slipped to keep off a slight drizzle. The hats and the view of the sea behind the spires of a tall cathedral were enough to make me realize that we had come to Brittany.

A few hours later, we reached the peninsula of Quiberon, and we finally arrived at a small village dominated by a huge bulky church. We walked past some shops, turned into a long road that led down to a beach, and, halfway down, stopped in front of a house that had white window frames and an orchard on the side. This was the house the family had rented for the summer. It was not very roomy, and, each evening, Jacques and I pushed aside the table and chairs in the living room and made beds for ourselves on the floor. We slept near an open window, and, in the late evening, when darkness was falling, the air was filled with the hum of insects and the chirping of cicadas.

Jacques and I did not get on well together. He plainly disliked me, and I found that his presence aroused no surge of enthusiasm within me. We were coolly polite to each other.

During the first days, we engaged in the usual pastimes of seaside tourists. We went to the beach, tried out the water, walked up and down, looked at everybody else doing the same things, and enjoyed the sunshine. At the dinner table, because I was a visitor, I was invited to help myself first when the courses were passed around. The menu, for the most part, consisted of things that could be put into one bowl or, at most, two. During my first evening, when the main bowl was passed to me, I picked out the spoon and helped myself. I took hardly more than one dessert spoonful and then decided that a second one was called for; as I reached across to take the second spoonful, I noticed Madame frowning horribly and looking pointedly at her husband and then at everyone else. I dropped the spoon and watched the bowl being passed around. I looked at the small helping of food on my rather large dish and came sadly to the conclusion that this was supper, the main meal of the day.

The following night, when the bowl was passed to me, I tried to guide the spoon in such a way as to get as much as possible and at the same time to land some of the solider parts of the food, such as lumps of meat. I had deposited these on my dish when the bowl was lifted by Madame and passed to somebody else, and the spoon, which was still in my hand, was requisitioned by one of the children beside me and passed on to catch up with the bowl. When I arose from the table, I was still hungry.

The next morning, I woke up late. As I came to, I slowly realized that the house was oddly quiet. I missed especially the sounds of the youngest child, who was so thoroughly spoiled that her presence was unmistakable in any house wherever she might be. I got up and looked out the window. It was a beautiful morning; the sun was already high; and the fields across from me were shimmering in the heat. I could make out, beyond them, the blue strip of seashore and, beyond that, the outline of cliffs. I walked out and looked around the house. Nobody was in sight. I retired to the bathroom, and, when I had finished there, I got dressed and went out into the back garden, where I found the maid, sitting on the back step. I asked where everybody was, and she said, "Oh, they all left for an excursion early this morning, about seven o'clock. They won't be back until tonight." She added, "They said to look after you. When you are hungry, come and tell me, and I'll give you some lunch."

I passed the day walking in the neighborhood. I went first to the harbor and watched the trawlers come in with their loads of fish, and I listened to the sailors as they came ashore with their blue berets and their canvas-colored clothes. They talked among themselves in Breton, which, although it is a Celtic language, is so completely different from Irish that I could understand nothing of what they said. I walked into the village, looked at the shops, and visited the big church, where the sunlight through the stained-glass windows spread over the gaunt pillars, the chairs, and the plain floor. Models of trawlers and schooners hung from the ceiling, and in one corner was an altar dedicated to Saint Anne, the patroness of Breton sailors, which was covered with little slabs, each one of them with a simple message, usually the one word *"Merci."* These were gifts and offerings brought to express gratitude for having come safely through some Atlantic storm. In one corner was the line *"Dieu prenne en pitié les bons matelots."* I thought of the sailors who had gone in their small boats and traveled the Atlantic routes in search of a livelihood, and of the women and old people left behind, who wondered if they would ever see them again. I could understand something of all this because, as I thought of them, I inevitably thought of my grandfather in Kerry and of others like him who had had to take to the sea in their canvas boats to supplement the meager livelihood available on land. There were orchards near the church, and I walked slowly past them and looked at the apples and the pears, the plums and the quinces. Then, I realized it was evening and time to go home and have a meal, for I was hungry, very hungry.

I went back to the house, and the family had returned. I was in time to join them at table. The bowl was placed in front of me; I helped myself to a spoonful; and the bowl was taken away again. I continued to live like this in the days that followed. The family would take off, and I would be left at home; the maid would prepare some lunch for me; and I would walk around the neighborhood, through the fields, and to the cliff tops, where I stood looking across to the blue line of Belle Ile on the horizon, watching the water and the birds and the small boats that occasionally came in.

Then, one day, I was confronted on the road by a gray-haired woman with glasses. I had seen her now and again, for she lived next door in the house with an orchard, and sometimes in the evening she and her husband used to sit in chairs on a sun porch beside the trees. She smiled at me and introduced herself.

"My name is Madame l'Hostis, and I hear you are the Irishman."

"Yes, I am indeed from Ireland," I said.

"Please come in," she said. "My husband would like you to come."

I followed her through a gateway into her house, and she brought me straight to the kitchen, where the table was laid. A place was set, and she said, "Please, won't you sit." And I sat. She put a large bowl of fresh prawns in front of me and some brown bread that she had made herself, and some fruit. She said, "Please eat." And I did; I ate everything in sight. When I had finished, she called her husband, and he came in, introduced himself to me, shook my hand, and welcomed me.

"We've been hearing about those barbarians who brought you here," he said. "The neighbors all think it a scandal the way they go off and leave you. Certainly, I will not rent the house to them again."

Everyday, Madame l'Hostis would find me somewhere and insist that I come in and have something to eat, and I was glad to do so, because, by then, I would have been hungry without her. Indeed, I had written to my parents a letter that did not disclose the full extent of my problem but that indicated that, if they sent me some chocolate and the like, it would be much appreciated. I had no money and could buy nothing for myself. The arrangement that had been made in Belvedere was that all the boys would be paid a certain amount of pocket money each week by the families with whom they stayed. No such money was ever given to me, and so I had nothing.

One night, when we came together for supper, the main item on the menu was fish. As usual, it was handed around. I took one and put it on my dish and ate it, and then, to my utter astonishment, I was invited a few moments later to have some more. I gladly did so. And the astonishment turned to wonder when I was invited to help myself again. It was only after I had eaten the third fish—they were fairly small, but I do not remember what they were—that I noticed that nobody else had eaten any. As I began to take note of that fact, a titter spread across the table, among the members of the family, and the joke was finally revealed. The fish had been left out too long after being caught and had begun to go bad. Everybody was in on the secret except myself, and giggles spread all around as I devoured one, and then a second, and then a third. Fortunately, I suffered no ill effects.

A few mornings later, the postman brought a parcel from Dublin. It contained a generous supply of chocolate, and, with this and the meals I had in the house of Madame l'Hostis, I was able to get by quite satisfactorily.

I roamed through the countryside, crossed the fields, and explored the cliffs. I took my books with me and read in the shadow of a medieval monastery. One day, I borrowed a bicycle and rode over to Carnac, where I walked among the rows of gigantic prehistoric pillars that stand there, silent puzzling remnants of lost eons. On my way back, the bicycle chain disintegrated and jammed into the back wheel so tightly that I was faced with the prospect of having to carry the machine the remaining miles to Quiberon. However, a Breton farmer who noticed me at the side of the road came over to see what was wrong, asked me if I was an Englishman, and, when I said no, that I was from Ireland, promptly picked up the machine, brought it into his house, and set to work repairing it for me. About half an hour later, I was able to jump on the seat and roll off down the highway, while the farmer leaned over his front gate and waved.

The next morning, I received a letter from Paris. It was from the Belvedere Jesuit who was the leader of the expedition and had come over with us from Dublin a few weeks before. My parents had grasped the fact that all was not well with me in Quiberon, and they had sent instructions that I was to be rescued. The letter to me said that I was to come back to Paris straightaway and that word was being sent to the man of the house to inform him of my departure.

I went to Paris, and the priest found a room for me in the house where he himself was a lodger. It was in Versailles. I borrowed money from him, and he gave me some maps and a phone number to call in case I got lost.

I was free.

Each morning, I set off from my room in Versailles and headed for Paris. I had no idea where I would go or what I would do. I drifted with the crowds and watched the

world go by. I walked by the Seine and stood behind the
men with their poles, as they cast, waited for a fish to bite,
and, meanwhile, passed the time with the puffing of a
cigarette or the lighting of a pipe. I strolled under the
bridges. I ambled across the gardens and along the side
streets and into the churches and museums and galleries. I
wandered into the Orangerie and the Jeu de Paume, to
discover for the first time what impressionism was, and I
came away and looked with new vision on Paris and the
scenes around me. I read the billboards, and, one day, I
discovered that I could see the Paris Passion Play.

I made my way to the Ile de la Cité, where an improvised
open-air theatre had been created in front of Notre Dame.
The traffic had been sealed off. On either side were trees
and beyond them were the multicolored façades of apartment houses. The roar of the distant traffic filtered through,
but it began to fade somehow as the old drama of the
Passion was enacted before us. The actors appeared on a
simple platform set up before the façade of Notre Dame.
There were no props of any kind—just the face of the
cathedral, lined and adorned with eight centuries of history.
As the various acts of the drama were performed, the outline of the cathedral became ever more sharply etched
against the darkening sky. At last came the climax. The
night had fallen; the stars were out; and the three crosses
were slowly raised; as they were, the rose window was
illuminated, and the gigantic bell began to peal. Time
seemed to pause, and there were the crosses and the full
glory of the rose window behind them, and from above
the tolling of the bell.

Then, abruptly, it was over, as floodlights were switched
on and the actors took their bows. The audience rose. There
was the shuffle of feet and the buzz of conversation. The
traffic on either side of the island resumed its noise. The

lights of the city were on. Before long, the only reminder of what we had seen was the continued massive presence of the cathedral.

The next day, I left Versailles as usual, but, this time, instead of keeping around the river and the museums and the gardens in the center of the city, I walked up toward Montmartre, along the streets that rose gradually, and then I climbed past flights of stairs, past apartment houses, and past the artists' quarters, until I reached the strange white building Sacré-Coeur. I walked inside and hoped to cool off there, for it was very hot. At last, I came out, not much refreshed, and I stood and looked across the long panorama of the city, which seemed to be trembling in the haze and the hot afternoon sun. As I did so, I noticed below me a small store that advertised Coca Cola. I knew what it was, but I had never tasted it, for it was not yet available in Ireland. So I resolved to continue my education by trying it, and, besides, the idea of an ice-cold drink was delectable. I went down, bought myself a bottle of it, with a straw, and came out and sat on a bench, still able to look across the rooftops and the spires, with the gleam of the sun on metal and windows and the shiver of heat stretching away as far as the horizon. As I began to sip my drink, a man came and sat beside me. He started by remarking that I must find this quite a contrast with England. I gave him that special frosty look that Irishmen reserve for foreigners who mistake them for Englishmen.

He asked me, *"Est-ce qu'il fait beau en Angleterre?"*

"Je n'en sais rien," I replied sourly.

"Mais vous venez de l'Angleterre, n'est-ce pas?"

"Non."

At this, he became interested. *"Alors, d'où venez-vous?"*

"Je suis irlandais," I told him.

"Ah, hollandais!"

"Non, irlandais."

"De quelle côté de l'Hollande?"

"Irlandais, pas hollandais."

"Irlandais?"

"Oui."

"Ah, bon." He decided to change the subject. "If I were you, I wouldn't drink that," he said.

"Why?" I asked, eying my half-consumed bottle of Coca Cola.

"Haven't you heard about the stuff they put in it?"

"No," I said.

"Why, it's a well-known international plot. An American plot. There's a drug in Coca Cola, and every time you take one, you get thirstier and you have to get more Coca Cola, and it becomes worse. Soon it becomes a fixation, a passion."

I was halfway through my Coca Cola, and I began to wonder. It was true. I was not feeling as refreshed as I should be, and in a few minutes I might have to run back to the store and buy another bottle. I could feel the thirst beginning to grow on me.

"It's a plot!" said the stranger. "We had to send our Foreign Minister to Washington to tell them to stop it. Ah, those Americans!" He got up, stretched, yawned, shook his head a few times, and walked away.

For a while, I sat and wondered whether I should finish my drink. But the heat got through to me, and I drank the last drops. By nightfall, I was satisfied that I had not become an addict.

And then my time began to run out. I hurried to walk once more along the Seine and to revisit the galleries where the impressionist paintings were gathered. I ate my supper by the river, my legs dangling over the bank. I ate croissants and drank juice and watched the barges, with their clotheslines at the back, moving up the river. I sniffed the dust and the hot air, and later, in the Luxembourg Gardens, I listened to the fountains and saw how lovers twined themselves around each other exactly like those depicted by the statues beside them. Still later, I stood petrified in the middle of the Champs Elysées, caught between the sidewalk and a traffic island, immobile, as cars whirled by on either side of me. I watched the crowds surging toward the Place de la Concorde, and I knew that I would soon be home and back at school and working and doing my lessons, and the dream would end.

On one of my last evenings, I went into the Royal Gardens in Versailles and sat in the midst of a large crowd. The sun had long since gone down. Over us came the sound of music. In the middle of one of the artificial lakes was a stage on which members of a ballet company were performing *Swan Lake*. The dancers seemed to be skimming over the water, and all the movement and the patterns and the beauty that they fashioned were played out against a backdrop of tall trees—rows of sturdy, ancient trunks that climbed to dark green leaves that reflected the lights from below and the first rays of the moon from above. All that night, my dreams were of white figures, exquisite as jewels, delicate as gossamer, whirling among tall trees and over leaping waters.

I caught myself dreaming of them again a few days later, as I sat in the plane that was taking us back to Ireland. We flew over Dublin Bay, circled once, and came into the airport; as we pulled up to the terminal building, one of my schoolmates behind me peered out the window and shouted excitedly, "My God! Look at the balcony! There are buckets of people there." I remembered suddenly that we would soon be back at Belvedere, back at another round of work and study.

21

Belvedere: The Last Two Years

My last two years were filled with essays and texts, languages and mathematics. The Debating Society and other school activities provided some distraction, as did the usual excitements of city life. When summer came, I returned to Versailles, where I passed many marvelous days and where, one evening, I was at a dinner party at which a Belvedere Jesuit was the guest of honor. We ate in a garden under trees, and the air was full of birds and the heat of the summer evening. At some point during the meal, one of the boys delivered a devastating attack on the Jesuits. Later on, when the Jesuit had gone home, the hostess took her son severely to task.

"Didn't you know he was a Jesuit?" she asked.

"No."

"Well, he was," she said. "That's why I gave you such a kick under the table after you made that remark."

"Kick?" said the boy, looking puzzled.

"You mean you didn't feel it?" asked the hostess. "I kicked you as hard as I could."

The rest of us were questioned, and, at last, the hostess was compelled to conclude that her aim was bad and that she had kicked the Jesuit.

When I returned from France and began my last year at school, I discovered that I had been selected to be one of the school prefects. We had some privileges, but, in return, we were expected to keep the day-to-day organization of the school running smoothly. We were also supposed to report on the conduct of the other students, and in the office of the Prefect of Studies was a notebook in which we were supposed to enter the names of students guilty of misdemeanors. It was a job I did not especially enjoy, another chore in addition to the many I already had. But the year went by speedily, and, at last, we found ourselves with the final examination to do. One afternoon, it was all over. The last question had been answered; the last paper, handed in. Since it is not customary in Ireland to have a ceremony on leaving secondary school, there would be no graduation ceremonies. For most, there would be a handshake, a word of farewell to a desk mate or a teacher, and then out through the gates into a new world, and a new life.

For a few of us, this moment was postponed because we had signed up to be members of the first of what would be an annual series of expeditions from Belvedere to Germany. Six of us, accompanied by two Jesuits, took knapsacks and sleeping bags, went to Cologne, and began a journey that was to take us south through Bavaria into Austria. We stayed in youth hostels, and, in Cologne, we were awakened each morning by a man who appeared in the corridor with a violin on which he played the German national anthem, following it up with a long, echoing *"Guten Morgen!"* We went to Bonn and Frankfurt and on south, and, as we went, we stayed in monasteries and convents, where, if we were not offered meals, we shamelessly scrounged them. Everywhere along the way, as far as Munich, we passed the ruins and rubble of the war that had ended eight years earlier.

We stopped one afternoon at a Franciscan monastery, where we admired the architecture and where we also lingered because it was lunchtime. The guest master came out to meet us. He spoke no English, and our collective knowledge of German was inadequate for effective conversation; so we had to settle for Latin. Eventually, he remarked that we must have eaten by then.

"Speramus" ("We have our hopes"), our leader said.

A smile passed over the face of the guest master, and then his beard stretched, as he began to guffaw.

"Speramus!" He chuckled, and, leading us to the refectory, where he fed us well, he laughed and shook his head, repeating over and over, *"Speramus, speramus!"*

We moved into the Bavarian Alps, amid forests and high mountains. We stayed in hostels and monasteries; we visited Oberammergau and entered Austria; and then we headed back toward Cologne. There were numerous incidents to fill the postcards we sent to our parents and friends. The father and two sons who spent several nights in the hostel at Benedictbeuern, who shook hands each night before going to sleep, and every morning when they awoke, lying side by side in the bunks, got up and shook hands again. The editor of the small-town paper who stood on the platform of the railway station one night, waving to us as the train pulled out and shouting after us, *"Gute Fahrt! Gute Fahrt!"* looking puzzled as we all burst into roars of laughter. The wine festival where we watched men walking in and crawling out. The night I got sick and seemed threatened with pneumonia. We got on a train; we had third-class tickets, but one of the priests told me to go up to the first-class carriage, settle in, and keep as warm and comfortable as possible. I did so; the ticket collector came; and I had nothing to give him. He asked me for my ticket several times in German, and I answered in Irish, which he, naturally, did not understand. He tried French, and I feigned ignorance of that language, too. He tried broken English. He tried combinations of all three. He went through the motions of producing tickets and punching them, and I smiled and replied in Irish that I had no first-class ticket, that I wasn't feeling very well, that I was sitting here, and that I did not know English. At last, he gave up and turned to the only other passenger in the compartment, an American Air Force captain, who had watched the proceedings with the greatest interest. The ticket collector went away, and, about half an hour later, the train began to pull into Frankfurt. I was not too sure; so I leaned across and asked the captain, "This is Frankfurt, isn't it?" He sat back, looked at me in astonishment, and then began to grin.

"Yes," he said.

"Good," I said. "I must be going." And I left him.

We took a boat trip along the Rhine, amid vineyards and old castles. Because it was afternoon and the sun was shining and the boat was rocking, we felt drowsy. We had our cameras but were too lazy to use them. We watched other, more zealous, tourists, and we felt the soothing touch of the breeze as the landscape floated by.

We noticed that there was a great scarcity of tea and

coffee, of which we had a considerable supply. Indeed, we had smuggled some in when we had come across by way of Belgium. We sold our tea at a price far above what we had paid for it and far below what it cost in Germany, and, on the proceeds, we took off for Nuremberg, where we wandered through the flattened, ruined streets and picked our way over bricks and rubble and stood enchanted before a Glockenspiel on an old church that was filled inside with the reminders of a very long past.

Then we were in Cologne again, and it was time to go. We headed back through Belgium and Holland to England and across the Irish Sea, until we stood one morning at Westland Row Station in Dublin and said good-by to one another.

That was the summer of 1953. My Belvedere days were over. I would carry away with me a host of memories over which to ponder. I had noticed that men of great gifts, who have undergone careful and prolonged training and who have read widely in many fields, run the serious risk of turning arrogant and all-knowing, of hearing instead of listening, of languishing in the unshakable conviction that they know what is best for others. At Belvedere I saw men of great talent who had survived this risk. They knew our nonsense to be nothing else, and yet they continued to talk across to us, not down. Some were kinder than others in the way they demolished ignorance, but behind and beyond it all was a certain humane tolerance, which pervaded the atmosphere of the school. There was something more, though I did not recognize it until many years later, when I watched the operations of other Jesuits in supposedly more advanced communities. It came to me then that I had been given the opportunity at Belvedere to see men who, despite any ambitions to be successful teachers, community leaders, or guides of public opinion, were, above all, moved by some continuing urge to be Christian. They seemed slightly more interested in service than in achievement, and, because this was so, they were capable of a degree of humanity utterly foreign to many of their colleagues elsewhere.

PART VI

RADIO EIREANN

22

The Routine

Often, throughout the 1940's and the 1950's, our letter slot at home would flap and an envelope addressed to me would fall onto the floor. Inside would be two sheets of blue paper. On top would be the words "Radio Eireann," and below would be the information that a play was to be performed—usually in Irish—at a date specified, that I was being offered a part, that my pay per performance would be five shillings, or U.S. $1 (later raised to seven shillings and sixpence, boosted eventually to thirty shillings), and that I should appear for rehearsals at the times stated on the back.

On the appointed day, I would go into town and get off

the bus at the GPO, turn the corner into Henry Street, and go up in the elevator to the third floor. From the elevator, one emerged into a lobby and then turned left through a frosted-glass door into a long corridor. If one had business at Radio Eireann, if he were famous, lowly, or just noisy, he had to traverse this corridor, which was tiled in white and prompted Sir Thomas Beecham, the famous musician, to describe it as the "longest entrance to a public latrine" he had ever encountered. From the offices along the corridor came a variety of sounds—an occasional typewriter, an animated conversation, a record being listened to by someone who had a program to prepare, a burst of laughter as the latest story went the rounds.

Some of the offices were quite large and furnished with a table and a collection of chairs. We would gather in one of these for the rehearsal of the latest play. The producer would arrive, distribute the scripts to the various persons involved, assign parts, and issue instructions, and we would begin a preliminary reading. Then we would be dismissed and, on another day, we would arrive again and, having traversed the corridor, go upstairs to one of the studios and have what was called the microphone rehearsal. In the studios, we would simulate a live broadcast, run through our play again once, twice, maybe more times, receive further instructions from the director, and, finally, await the hour when it was time to go on the air.

I had been introduced to this special and rather marvelous world by my father. He had made his first broadcast in 1932, when he had read a short story of his own and had earned ten shillings (or U.S. $2.50) for his labors. Because he was deeply interested in the theater and in acting, he became increasingly involved with radio as well, where he took part in plays, wrote some, and came more and more to specialize in directing. He seemed to get the most satisfaction from his role as a director, and, even if I had no part in a production for which he was responsible, I would often go with him and sit in his cubicle to watch him at work.

He would sit with turntables on either side. In front of him were a microphone and a set of signal lights. To his left was a window, on the other side of which was the balance-and-control room, and, at a panel beyond the window sat the balance-and-control engineer, who had a desk and knobs and buttons with which he controlled the volume, the signals, the transmission, and other aspects of broadcast sound. There had to be constant communication between the director and the balance-and-control man, but this had to be carried out exclusively by sign language. So my father would drop a needle on a record, his hand would rise in a dramatic sweep straight up toward the ceiling, and the balance-and-control man would turn the music on suddenly and full. Or, over another record, my father would let his hand hover and make patting motions, and over the air would come the faint distant sound of music; then, my father's hand would turn at an angle and slowly begin to rise, and the distant music would begin to come closer; as my father's hand rose to shoulder level and climbed higher, the music would take over and fill the air. Sometimes, he would have two records going simultaneously, and, with one hand, he would urge the sound of one forward while the other hand would hold the second one in check, and the balance-and-control man would watch carefully so that his hands would respond to any signal that my father had given him. Jerks with thumbs and forefingers would mean that my father wanted one studio put on the air, or perhaps two together. When a particular effect had been achieved to his satisfaction, my father would beam at the man at the other side of the window and raise both thumbs.

Since the appeal of radio is to the ear and, ultimately, to the imagination, much depended on the director, not only to coach the actors to bring forth every nuance in the play but also to devise the sound effects that would convey to the listening audience what was going on. In the 1940's, there was no such thing as a professional sound-effects man, and, in the production of the plays, we had to rely heavily on the imagination of the director and also on the various devices that littered the studio.

We did a play once whose scene was a boat that got caught in a storm at sea, with disaster to all hands. There was no record available that would suggest the gradations of wind; so we had to rely on a gadget that was kept in one of the main studios. It was a wooden, octagonal device resting on a trestle and with a handle, like a crank handle, at one side. A length of canvas was stretched over the top of this octagonal device, and, when you turned the handle, the octagon revolved at whatever speed you desired. When you turned the handle gently, the friction on the canvas produced a gentle sound, like the murmur of a breeze. Speed it up, and you got a rising wind; whirl it around, and you got a full gale. An actor not currently on the air would bend over the device, carefully watching his script, which he held in one hand while he whirled the octagon at full speed with the other hand. Bent over and trying to combine the reading of his script with the production of a hurricane, he often presented a fine sight, perspiring at the job and trying to make sure that the gale stopped at the right moment.

In many of our plays, a door had to be opened or shut, a letter had to be delivered, somebody had to knock, or, sometimes, a hero would stalk out in anger and slam a door behind him. For all of these effects, we had a wooden box about four and a half feet high, with a door attached to it.

The door had hinges that could be made to creak or not, as the play required; it had a knocker, a bolt, a letterbox, a bell, and a latch. It had two locks, one small and one big, with a small key and a big key. If the play called for the great door of an old mansion, the bigger key was used. But if the play concerned an ordinary house door with an ordinary housewife turning the key, then the smaller one was employed. By slamming the door (and thus closing the box), one could produce the reverberation that suggested the idea of stalking out of a room in anger.

Sometimes, we had to add to our stormy scenes a touch of thunder. For this, we had a long sheet of tin, and some actor who was not on the air at the moment would pick it up and shake it in front of the microphone, and it would shiver and produce the appropriate thunderous sounds. These sounds could also come unexpectedly, as happened during one broadcast: An actor who was backing away from the microphone, most effectively creating the impression of a man leaving a field, backed straight into the sheet of tin and knocked it over. It hit the grand piano and fell on the floor. There was thunder everywhere.

We had a play, another time, in which there was a talking whale. The whale had not merely to produce speech but also to suggest his natural surroundings, and, for this, we had a large bowl of water and a straw, and it was left to the imagination of the actor involved to produce the necessary sounds while his colleague who was playing the whale tried to adapt his voice accordingly.

In another play, a thoroughly nasty character was being pursued by the hero. They were out in an open field. He broke away and started to run. The hero shouted, "Stop! Stop, or I'll shoot!" and the other man continued to run. So two effects were required—the fugitive's running and the shot that brought him down. For the first, we had a box in which were little pebbles, and one actor held the box close to the microphone and ran two fingers around inside the box, thus rustling the pebbles and producing the scraping sound of a man out in the open air running down a gravelly road. Another actor had to pick up a box containing about two handfuls of dried peas and shake the box in the necessary manner. The result was not merely the sound of a shot but also the "ping" that goes with a bullet as it flies through the air. The fugitive then gave a cry of pain, and it was up to the listeners to visualize his collapse on the grass.

Frequent in the serials was the old stand-by, the pursuit. When it was not a pursuit by car, which could be managed by the director with records, it was usually a chase on horseback. For this, we had a series of hollowed-out semi-circles of wood, covered with inner tubing. Two of these clapped together at an angle could produce the sound of a horse's hooves; the speed with which one clapped regulated the speed of the horse. If several horses were involved, several actors would have to help out, and there would be the spectacle in the studio of men who did not have to speak at that particular moment, scripts tucked under their arms, each holding a pair of these pieces of wood and clapping them, moving away from the microphone, some in hot pursuit, some at a canter, some going at breakneck speed.

Sometimes, there would be an unrehearsed and unexpected effect. One evening, an actor who was badly affected by both nervousness and a hangover came too close to the microphone with his script. I could see the director in his cubicle as he sat up straight and began listening intently, for over the air was coming the sound of falling leaves. He came running over to the window and signaled frantically for someone to pull the actor away so that the shaking sheets of his script would not rustle so clearly.

Once, too, an actor who had two pages before his next speech went off to the men's room and reappeared two lines before he was due. He opened the studio door from the corridor outside, and the transition into the warmer and stuffier room caused him to sneeze violently before he could stop himself, and over the air came a loud "AH-choo!"

In one of our plays, there was a scene in which a donkey had to chew a mouthful of hay. There was no device in the studio with which to produce this effect. My father was directing the play, and it happened that, at this particular point, he had no records to put on or signals to deliver. So, at a prearranged signal, we pulled open the door of his cubicle at the appropriate moment, and he ran across to the microphone, stood in front of it, and chewed his false teeth briefly. The effect that came over quite adequately conveyed the sound of a donkey having a thoroughly satisfactory meal. Then my father ran back to his cubicle, picked up his records, and carried on with his work.

Later on, this aspect of our job was taken over by a professional sound-effects man appointed by the radio station. The first holder of this office had worked, I think, with a traveling circus and had operated under the name of Mervani the Magician. He enlivened many of our rehearsals and broadcasts with the tricks he was able to combine with his chores. One Saturday morning, we badly needed a record of shepherds, and Mervani and I were given the job of producing one. He got a record of a flock of sheep; we went into one of the studios; and the balance-and-control man gave us a partially opened microphone. We then stood around, shouting, "Hup! Go on there! Go on! Carry on!" and, while we yelled all this, Mervani performed some of his tricks for me. He showed me a cigarette and then it popped into his ear. He pushed it, and it disappeared inside his head and reappeared a moment later on his bald spot. He had, of course, the usual magician's ability to make things disappear, which could sometimes be frustrating. As an actor would reach for a cigarette to take a last quick drag before going on the air, he would find that it had vanished to another part of the studio, where it could not be reached but was smoking away in full view of the poor man who needed a pull but hadn't the time to run over and get it. Mervani would also mislay a thumb or a finger as he was casually crossing the studio or handing something to an actor. And he had tricks with bits of string, which he carried in his pockets and with which he sometimes diverted us during a few dull moments in a rehearsal.

In each studio, there was usually only one microphone, and it was quite an elaborate affair. A long bar, the middle of which rested on a movable tripod, had the microphone suspended from it at one end; at the other end was a heavy knob that acted as a counterweight for balance. The tripod could be wheeled around the studio, and the advantage of the bar was that the microphone could be lowered or raised to suit the needs of individual actors. We did *Oliver Twist*, and I played the role of Oliver. At a crucial moment in the play, there is a dramatic dialogue when the Beadle confronts Oliver and asks, "Oliver, ain't you quakin' in yer boots?" and Oliver looks boldly up at him and replies, "No, sir." By the time we did this play, I was already a six-foot tall, lanky youth, and the man who played the Beadle was well under five feet. When our confrontation came, a compromise was struck, and the microphone was hung down halfway between us, so I had to speak down into it while he spoke up into it.

The tripod also had some disadvantages. There was the famous night when an actor, finding the studio too hot, took off his jacket during a broadcast and flung it over the end of the arm, where the counterweight was, causing the microphone to shoot up to the ceiling. The result was an excruciating shriek. Balance-and-control men jumped on their panels and cut everything off the air, but, meanwhile, in the four corners of Ireland many astonished listeners wondered if their radio sets were blowing up.

The poor man responsible for this catastrophe seemed to be accident-prone. A few weeks earlier, he had a part in a play whose plot hung on the fact that a key event was to take place in the early morning, at a particular time. He was asked, in the play, what time it was, and the whole play depended on the answer he was to give—that it was nine in the morning. On the evening of the broadcast, when the question was put to him, he glanced at the studio clock and said, "Oh, it's five to seven," thus rendering the play entirely pointless. For a while thereafter, there was a ban on his presence in Radio Eireann.

If the motto of the theater is that the show must go on, the commanding imperative of radio is that there must never be silence. Sometimes, the danger of an unexpected silence was real. A man would miscalculate the amount of time he had before he must appear at the microphone to speak, and he would go outside to the corridor to have a quick smoke, or to go to the men's room, or even to have a quick drink at the Tower Bar, across the street. The moment would come when his lines would have to be delivered, and he would be nowhere in sight, and someone else would have to leap into the breach and take over for him until he arrived breathless and flushed from wherever he had been.

An actress in one play we were doing was facing one of the big studio windows. She could see the Dublin skyline outside, and, when a flash of lightning crossed it, she dropped her script in terror and got ready to run. It also happened that she was supposed to be delivering her lines, and a man nearby had to take over and produce his best imitation of a woman's voice and sound appropriately feminine until she had recovered her poise. Sometimes, the actors who were not performing would gather at the back of the studio and engage in whispered conversation; someone would crack a joke, and an actor who had to speak his part would be overcome by a paroxysm of laughter and become speechless. Someone else would have to take over for him until he recovered. Occasionally, a performer would fall asleep, unnoticed by the others, and, when his moment to speak came, he would be peacefully curled up at the back of the studio; so someone else would have to jump in and take over. I did this once for a man who was playing the role of an elderly king, and I had to try to reproduce with my teenage voice the deep tones of an old man who was advising his daughter, the princess, about the course of life she ought to pursue.

23

The Players

Most of those who took part in the plays on Radio Eireann in the 1940's and early 1950's were, like my father, members of other professions. There were quite a few school-teachers, because they had the advantage of a working day that ended in the early afternoon, giving them time to attend rehearsals and to be on hand for broadcasts from five o'clock onward. There were lawyers who were without work, civil servants who were supposed to be elsewhere, and some professional actors who depended on radio work for survival. There was no television; the opportunities of appearing in films were still quite limited; and the pay for appearing on stage was meager. Therefore, many actors were grateful to men like my father who employed them.

One man, in particular, was frequently sought by my father to play parts. He was a civil servant and, naturally, was not supposed to appear during the working day for rehearsals or for the recording of broadcasts or, indeed, for the live broadcasts that took place before five-thirty. He and I had a standing arrangement whereby I would phone him two pages before he was due to perform. He would disappear from his desk to go to the men's room or head off with a file under his arm, duck out a side door, run up across the center of Dublin, cross two main streams of traffic, run into Henry Street, and go up in the elevator, or, if the elevator had just left, he might have to run up the three flights of steps to the top. He would then have to traverse the long corridor, go up another flight of stairs, and burst into the studio a few lines before he was due to appear. I would be waiting for him with a script and with my finger pointing to the appropriate spot.

When these figures from varying backgrounds gathered together, there was usually much talk and plenty of laughter. I have a persistent recollection of pleasant encounters with pleasant individuals. They had their foibles and their off days, but they seemed, too, to have a capacity to turn routine tasks into occasions of fun, and, even if the object of their work was to earn some extra money, they seemed to enjoy to the full the numerous capers they had to perform. Around these figures and behind them were others who drifted in and out or played important parts in the setting up of the programs and the plays.

There were programs other than plays to put on. There were radio digests, discussion panels, short stories, quiz programs, and the like. One of the more successful of these, in which my father was involved, was a weekly musical program, which ran for a number of years and which brought my father together with an old friend, a man named Seamus Kavanagh. The program was a music quiz whose format provided plenty of opportunity to listen to music. The master of ceremonies put questions to opposing teams and chatted with them, and the listener was entertained with the mild perplexity imposed by questions of identification. My father was responsible for the choice of music, the choice of questions, and the direction of the program. For the talk, Seamus Kavanagh was responsible. And there were few men better equipped for the task.

Kavanagh had once been a schoolteacher, and, in the early 1930's, he, like my father, had been involved in the acting and production of plays in the Abbey and other theaters in Dublin. My father had given him his first part in a play, and that was the beginning of a long association. After performing this first part, Kavanagh was given a role in a play for which my father had no responsibility. The second part was very brief—he had to appear in the third act, knock at a door, be admitted, deliver a message, then withdraw from the stage. On the first night, the boredom of hanging around, waiting for the third act, combined with a certain nervousness, impelled Kavanagh to leave the theater to go to a neighboring pub to acquire a little fortification. In the process, he acquired a little too much fortification, and, when he returned to the theater, it was with only the vaguest notion of what he was to do there. He appeared on stage at the right moment, but, instead of knocking at the door and walking in, he crawled in on his hands and knees, delivered his lines, and proceeded to make his exit from the stage by crawling through a fireplace that was part of the décor.

"It was when I came through the fireplace that it hit me," he told me, many years later, recalling the incident. "I became cold stone sober in a flash. And then I crept away. And I met your father the following morning and he said to me, 'If I'd been the producer, I'd have kicked you from one end of O'Connell Street to the other.'

"And mind you, I was a bit annoyed with him for the way he said it. And then when people saw me coming they'd begin to laugh and go about their business. More and more people began to do this. They'd see me coming and there'd be a roar of laughter. It was only then that I began to realize that what your father had said to me was the kindest comment of all. O God, O God!" He would shake his head and pat the sizable paunch that he carried on his short legs.

But his misadventure did not interrupt his career. He appeared on stage in variety shows and in plays. He eventually abandoned his profession as a teacher and took on a job with Radio Eireann. By the end of the war, he was getting parts in films. Increasingly, calls would come from London, from the BBC, to go over and act in various plays. As he worked more, his popularity grew, for he was not only a very good and intelligent actor but also a very good and gentle man, whose wit was admired and whose stories, mostly directed against himself, were cherished by people who laughed with him and not at him.

"I woke up in the morning in the hotel and I knew it was time for me to go; so, I got up and shaved and got dressed and I went downstairs to the boy at the desk and said I'd come to pay the bill. He gave me the bill, and I paid him, and then he said, 'Mr. Kavanagh, and what about the cow?'

" 'What cow?' I asked.

" 'Your cow, Mr. Kavanagh.'

" 'I haven't got a cow!'

" 'Well, the one you bought last night, Mr. Kavanagh.'

" 'What are you talking about?'

" 'Well, you bought a cow from a farmer when you

were out at the pub last night, Mr. Kavanagh, and you brought it home and left it out at the back. What am I going to do with it?'

" 'O God. Look, son, will you take care of it for me?' And I slipped him some money.

" 'That'll be all right, Mr. Kavanagh; I'll see to it.' "

He spoke fondly, from time to time, of the role of a priest that he had played in a film shot out in Howth. The work had been long, and, at the end of a particularly tiring sequence, when he was hot and bothered, Seamus decided to slip out of the studio for a break. He was wearing a soutane and a biretta; he had not had time to change his costume. He ordered a pint of stout, and he stood by the side of one of the main roads leading into Howth, with one foot propped up on a barrel of Guinness and the pint in his hand, his biretta pushed to the back of his head. He sipped his drink and looked over the scenery and relaxed for a few moments from the rigors of work. As he was doing so, there was a squeal of brakes, and a car that had passed came back into view, reversing rapidly. Three clerics were in it, and one of them jumped out, shouting, "In the name of God, Father, what do you think you're doing? Think of the scandal!"

Kavanagh rarely visited our house, and there was one memorable night when, having been invited, he forgot to come. My mother had prepared an elaborate dinner and had been cooking for many hours. We hung around in the dining room for quite a while, but there was no sign of our guest. Finally, my father, suspecting he knew where Kavanagh was, called him. Kavanagh was summoned to the phone, was duly apologetic, and promised to catch a taxi and be out as soon as possible. By that time, the dinner was spoiled. When he arrived at the house, he apologized profusely to my mother, grinned at my father, shook my hand

and said, "You know, when your old man spoke to me on the phone there a while back, it was like listening to ice cubes tinkling inside a glass." As invariably happened, once in his presence, there was nothing we could hold against him. Before the night was out, my mother was wiping tears from her eyes, my father likewise, and I had an ache in my ribs from laughing.

He talked on, and, at one point, in the early hours of the morning, he began to describe a visit he had made to the Aran Islands off the west coast of Ireland, in the 1930's. He had been there often and, indeed, was later to make the trip an annual one. He was evidently as popular there as elsewhere. But he went on to describe a scene one morning when he had gone with all the islanders down to the harbor on Inis Mor to bid farewell to two young people who were emigrating to the United States. In those days, parents bidding their children farewell had no real expectation of seeing them again. Kavanagh spoke of the tears among the women and of the moment when a father said good-by to his son. He rose from his chair in our dining room and went through the motions of embracing a son; for a brief instant, we found ourselves on a quayside on an Atlantic island while an old man, filled with pained, wordless grief, bade his child good-by.

Everywhere he went, Kavanagh was remembered for being kindly and thoughtful, and most of all for the pleasure he had evoked around him. But, as the years went on, he carried an increasing burden of sadness within him. For, amid the laughter and the success, the films, the many parts, the stories, the all-night sessions of brilliant talk with men of great talent, Kavanagh was a lonely man. He knew my father sensed it, and he knew my father's compassion for him. Weeks, sometimes months, might pass without their meeting. But I always had a distinct feeling that, when they did meet, it was for Kavanagh not simply another of many encounters, just as for my father it was clearly a chance to be once more with a deeply cherished friend. Kavanagh continued to laugh and to talk with enthusiasm. He became Director of Children's Programs on Radio Eireann. On the radio, he played Captain Boyle in O'Casey's *Juno and the Paycock* with the special insight born of his Dublin years. To Joyce's Leopold Bloom he brought a gravel-voiced, sad ennui, which was just right for that special brand of comedy whose roots are ultimately tragic. On Saturday mornings in the late 1950's, when I had come back on summer vacations from Princeton, where I was a student, I used to go with my father into the center of Dublin to the Tower Bar to meet Kavanagh, and we would stand at the counter, and the talk and the laughter would continue for hours.

Then, in the early 1960's, word came that Kavanagh was sinking, and, one evening, the news came that he was dead, and I knew that I was one of many who felt a very deep sorrow. My father was at Radio Eireann that same evening, in charge of the rehearsal of a play. Halfway through the rehearsal, word was brought that Kavanagh was dead. My father threw aside his script, dismissed his actors, and went home.

There were few at Radio Eireann whom I got to know as well as Seamus Kavanagh, but, still, when I appeared at rehearsals and the director handed out the scripts and as-signed the characters and the parts and issued his customary instructions, it was a pleasure to look around the rehearsal room and see the many familiar faces and to see the many whom I had come to know over a period of years, who had in their own way shown kindness and understanding to me. During many years we had collaborated to make serious business fun.

In the summer of 1956, I ended my association with Radio Eireann. By that time, I was a university student, and all my days were filled with the thought of the examination for the degree, which was only a matter of months ahead of me. A great stroke of luck came my way. A serial that had been highly successful the previous year was repeated. It was a children's program describing the adventures of a boy and some animal friends—a donkey, a dog, a cat, and a rooster—who traveled around together, spoke with one another, and sang songs whenever the mood struck them (which was at least three times every program). In that summer, when the pressures of final exams were building up, I was given a part in the first episode of the series. At the end of this episode, some roles had to be switched around, and I was given one of the leading parts—that of a singing, talking, cackling rooster. Each week for fourteen weeks I was able to look forward to the prospect of forgetting completely the world of study and exams and of entering for four or five hours into a different environment, where a group of us gathered together in front of a microphone with our scripts and our instructions, to sing, talk, cackle, and laugh in a world of make-believe. We sang our songs and conducted our adventures, in which we had trying encounters with goats and ducks and an occasional aberrant human being.

If any of my professors had chanced to have a radio on at that moment and had heard a chorus which concluded with the words, "Hee-haw, hee-haw, and bow-wow, meow!" and had listened briefly to the lusty cock-a-doodle-do that followed this chorus, would the thought ever have occurred to him that among these were the tones of a candidate for a bachelor's degree at the autumn exams? It did not even occur to me to wonder about this; for the beauty of it all was that I had only one task now at this particular moment, and that was to express, heart and lungs, the convictions of a rooster.

PART VII

DUBLIN 3

24

Statues, the Grand Piano, and Bang-bang

When I stand on O'Connell Bridge looking up to where Nelson's Pillar used to be or watch the flow of the Liffey as it comes down to the Ha'penny Bridge, passes underneath, and goes out the other side and on under Butt Bridge, out past the Customs House and out to the sea, I find images of earlier days crowding into my mind, of days when I stood here on the bridge or walked across as a schoolboy or traipsed along, holding my mother's hand as she went about her business.

For instance, there were the Guinness barges that set off from near Kingsbridge and came downriver, painted blue with a tall orange-red funnel and loaded with barrels of stout. The funnel had to be lowered as the barge passed under O'Connell Bridge, and a man sat beside it and waited until the very last instant before unclipping it and laying it on its back. Smoke would scatter in all directions; the barge would emerge on the other side; and the man would put the funnel up again.

At the corner of the bridge, there stood for years a man with a pianola. He had his hat in his right hand, and with his left he turned the handle and out came the tunes, old and shaky. There was Johnny Fortycoats, long since dead, whose bulky figure used to amble slowly across the bridge. He had a gray hat and mouse-colored whiskers, and he shuffled along, wearing many layers of clothing. I counted three coats on him one day; on another, four. Under these, he had shirts and sweaters. There were the photographers on the bridge, who walked up and down trying to keep warm in winter. They raised their cameras as you approached and seemed to be on the point of taking a picture. Sometimes, they did take one and handed you a slip of paper as you walked by, but I rarely saw them doing enough photography to convince me that they were making much of a living. Yet, they stayed there year after year, and, with the passage of time, their faces got redder and their noses more purple.

There was the sound of a bell rung by a man outside one of the furniture stores along Bachelor's Walk. He was announcing an auction. From one of these auction rooms came the piano that was found one day to be a nuisance and was carried by the owner across the road and dumped over the wall into the Liffey, so that, when the tide was out and the river low, one could see the grand piano resting on the mud. It was in one of these same rooms that a friend of the family's bought a grandfather clock and was seen staggering up Bachelor's Walk with it. At the corner of the bridge he was observed by two Dubliners, one of whom remarked to the other, "Wouldn't you think he'd get himself a wristwatch?"

There is the tall, elaborate statue of Daniel O'Connell: One day, when I was small, I stood behind a man who was deeply troubled by something and who raised a finger to Dan and denounced and harangued him and told him that his view of Ireland and of history had been distorted and wrong. I noticed that passers-by paid no attention to the man, and, of course, they were right, for he was by no means the first to stand on the bridge and address the tall, silent figure above him. Below Dan O'Connell are seated four angelic female figures. I walked behind two women, one day, and one of them said to the other, "Wouldn't you think, after all these years, they'd cover that thing up?" For a moment I was puzzled, until I realized that she was referring to the female figure whose breast had a bullet hole through the nipple, a bullet hole that is a legacy of the 1916 uprising.

Daniel O'Connell is a reminder of the very many other statues throughout the city. There was one that I watched for years as a boy and on through my university days, and which I still pause to look at whenever I am passing by. It is the statue of Tom Moore. He stands with his back to an underground toilet, and some element in his metal causes the statue to lose its blackish-brown color and to acquire brown patches out of which eventually come moldy green stripes, until at last the Dublin Corporation is compelled to paint him over once again. For years I watched him. He was regularly repainted, and, for a few weeks, he would stand shining and splendid, and then the patches would begin to reappear as though he had a persistent brand of mange. He holds a notebook in one hand and in the other a pencil, hovering over a page. For years that pencil has been a godsend to countless groups that wanted to advertise their activities to the city. Regularly Tom Moore would have a notice hanging from his pencil, that a dance would be held at a certain place and time, or urging passers-by to vote for a particular candidate in an election.

As you go by him and pass the railing of Trinity College, there is, on the other side, the statue of Henry Grattan. He has one hand raised, with the index finger pointing, and his fingers are extended as he emphasizes an argument. I always looked at those fingers as I passed by him, because, from time to time, he conjured something out of the air— a liqueur glass, a beer tankard, a sheet of paper, a notice of a dance.

In the Phoenix Park there was the statue of Lord Gough, which I passed occasionally and which I always admired— a regal figure on a prancing steed, and he was always in trouble. One morning someone would find that one of the horse's legs had been sawn off. There would be a search, and, eventually, the missing part would be found and stuck back on. Lord Gough lost his head one day. It, too, had been sawn off, and, for a long time, the headless statue graced the entrance to the park. Then, one day, a terrific explosion shook the city, and, when the guards hurried to investigate, they found that Lord Gough and his horse had been transformed into a fine downpour of metal.

On Marlborough Street, near my father's school, there was a very big statue of a nineteenth-century figure who had been connected with the world of education. He was sitting on a chair; he had his back to the schools and to the offices belonging to the Department of Education; and he looked through the thick railing to the Procathedral across the road. From time to time, when I was a boy (for the statue has since disappeared), I used to see a man curled up in the lap of this imposing figure, enjoying a peaceful sleep.

When I walked past this statue and turned along the flank of the Procathedral and came out again onto O'Connell Street, I would sometimes stand at the corner and watch the news vendor who sat on a box under a clock, his newspapers beside him. He was blind, and, when a customer handed him a coin for which change was required, the news vendor would feel each coin with his fingers quickly and expertly and complete the transaction. Opposite him and in the middle of the road behind Nelson's Pillar was a line of trees, and, at night, I used to stop sometimes and look up at the countless thousands of wagtails that gathered there, filling the air with their twittering and leaving a liberal distribution of birdlime on any cars that unwary Dubliners had parked nearby.

Frequently, as I was coming back from Belvedere after school, and was walking down past the Parnell Monument and had entered O'Connell Street and was moving toward the Pillar, a small figure in a raincoat, a man in his thirties, with his forelock slipping over his eye, would dash out at some corner, point an old iron door key at a car or a bus, and shout, "BANG! You're shot!" And he would do so in a voice of astonishing power, which could be heard clearly above the roar of the traffic. He was a familiar sight, and Dubliners knew him as "Bang-bang." He would leap onto the platform of a passing bus, and, hanging on the rail with one hand, he would shoot the cars behind him. When he was satisfied that he had shot enough of them, he would swing off, run to the other side of the street, and get a bus going in the opposite direction, leaving death and destruction around him everywhere.

One afternoon, I was coming down past the Gresham Hotel, where four Americans were standing and talking. Bang-bang came up behind them and fired at them. With a marvelous and instantaneous understanding, the four

Americans scattered and hid behind cars or behind pillars at the entrance to the hotel lobby. They fired back at Bang-bang. He had to take shelter in a doorway. A great duel took place there on O'Connell Street, and, eventually, the Americans, good sportsmen that they were, allowed themselves to be shot one by one. When he had downed all four of them, Bang-bang scurried across the pavement, hid behind a car for a moment, and then leapt onto a passing bus, hung from the platform, and shot down all the posses that had been organized to get him. Over the traffic noise rang his booming cry, "Bang! Bang! You're all shot!"

I would cross O'Connell Bridge into Westmoreland Street and move up past Bewley's coffee house, where the smell of freshly ground coffee came out to tempt passers-by, on toward the massive pillars of the Bank of Ireland, which used to be a spot favored by pavement artists and which, in more recent years, has attracted evangelists; on under the pillars and past the bank's parking lot, whose attendants wore special uniforms and black silk top hats. If I went up Dame Street, it might well be to find myself in some of the alleys and narrow streets and courtyards of an earlier era—in Fishamble Street, where the first performance of Handel's *Messiah* took place; in Hoey's Court, where Swift was born; in Crown Alley; or in Merchant's Arch, from whence I came out onto Burgh Quay and the Ha'penny Bridge.

Sometimes, catching the voice of Bang-bang over the traffic, or returning in the afternoon from Belvedere and making my way home, the thought would occur to me that the character of the traffic in the city had been changing since the days when I was first old enough to notice what was going on. As a child I used to watch with endless fascination the trolleys that rolled along to Nelson's Pillar from various points in the city. They moved along streets whose cobbles and rails have since disappeared. At corners, they screeched painfully as they slowed to go around. They were double-decker trolleys, and, at the front, the driver would stand before a metal column about three feet wide and perhaps four and a half feet tall. He had two metal handles, which would move up and down, and the trolley would speed up or slow down according to the signal he gave. Beside his foot was something that looked like a brake pedal stuck there just to get it out of the way, and, when the driver wished to give warning of his coming, he would dance on this, and there would come out from the bowels of the trolley a great clanging noise whose meaning was unmistakable. These trolleys would converge on Nelson's Pillar, and, as they came and crossed a network of points, the long arms reaching up to the wires would seem to explode at the tips like a match, and the arms would fall and begin to wave in the wind as the trolleys ground to a halt. The conductors would have to come out and take hold of two lines and try to persuade the recalcitrant arm to get back on the wires again.

Buses increasingly competed with the trolleys. There were the buses belonging to the Dublin United Transport Company, and there were also private buses such as the blue-and-white ones belonging to Andy Clarkin, which used to leave from Stephen's Green and head off in the general direction of Wicklow, stopping wherever and whenever anybody had a mind for them to do so. Then, the cobbles were torn up and the trolley tracks with them, and the green double-decker buses took over. At last, only a few trolleys were to be seen, not on the roads but in fields here and there around the neighborhood of Dublin, where someone had put one to serve as a home or a shed or even as a sort of greenhouse.

There were very few cars on the road during the war

years, and, even in the 1950's, the streets of Dublin swarmed with bicycles. One Saturday midday, I was standing in line, waiting for a bus, when I saw a man riding by on a penny-farthing. I had never seen one before, except in pictures, and I have seen only one or two since, in museums. The front wheel of the bicycle was about six feet in diameter; the rear wheel, perhaps two feet. A man perched on the top and rode through the city, and I was not alone in staring after him with pleasure and surprise.

I had my own bicycle, and I frequently rode to and from school on it. One day, when I was riding home, my front wheel lodged in one of the old trolley tracks. I was thrown in the air and fell on my back in the middle of the road. As I rolled over, I caught sight of the wheels of a car that had screeched to a halt a few inches away. It was the closest I had come to being a former Dubliner.

2 5

Christmas in Dublin

In the two or three weeks preceding Christmas, I used to walk down Henry Street to see and hear the vendors who came with their wares. They stood in a line, along the edge of the pavement, and they had wooden stalls on which they had decorations and toys and flares and dolls and all the things one might want to buy for Christmas. They shouted, "Sixpence a yard, the decorations!" or "Gitcher last jumpin' mouse!" or "Starlights, shillin' a packet!" They shouted to the passers-by all day, and their shouts seemed to grow into a great chorus in the hours just before six o'clock.

Around the corner from them, in Moore Street, stood

the women who for years had been selling oranges and apples, bananas and flowers, vegetables and fish. They stood at their wooden stalls and cried their wares in the accents unique to Moore Street and certain areas like it in Dublin. The women often looked dowdy and poor, but, as you got to know them better, it became increasingly clear that many of them were affluent. They stood out in all kinds of weather and shouted their prices, and, when it was time for a break, they slipped over to Jerry O'Dwyer's pub for whiskey or stout or both, and, in the middle of the day, many of them ate something known as "coddle," which is a kind of stew of potatoes, onions, rashers, and other ingredients. They washed it down with more stout or hot tea or a jigger of whiskey. One of them, quite famous, had a son who was in his forties when I first got to know him, and she used to bring him along like a small schoolboy. From time to time, he evidently displeased his mother; for she would interrupt her shouts of "Oranges, lemons!" to give him a tongue-lashing that blistered the air, and he listened to it as he had often had to listen before—silently and with his head hung down. Another woman stood farther up, short but of gigantic girth. She wore an apron over her coat, and she always carried some change in her right hand, on which there were two thumbs.

Christmas was also the season of pantomimes, which were put on in most of the theaters in the city. Onto a very simple, usually romantic, plot would be grafted spectacles to delight the eye and ear, and more important, perhaps, numerous sequences in which there would be vigorous satire whose targets included the politicians, the public corporations, and the current news stories. Some of the targets were hardy perennials of which Dubliners never seemed to tire. There was the American Ph.D. student doing a thesis on Joyce, always a figure of fun. There was the Kildare

Street Club, which until the 1950's was a haven for retired officers of the British Army, who seemed to come into decibel range sooner than most and who gathered over drinks and the London *Times* to talk of past glory.

Among the creators of pantomime, my favorite was Jimmy O'Dea, who put on a show at Christmas and at other times in the year as well. He was a small man, scarcely five feet high, and he was bald. He had brilliant brown eyes and the most eloquent eyebrows I have ever seen on any man.

"Did you see my Hamlet? Did you see my Lear? Did you see my Macbeth?" asked the tall impersonator of a famous actor.

"And did you see my Bottom?" asked Jimmy. A mildly amusing line, but, because he was Jimmy, and because he raised his eyebrows in a certain way, because he had drawn himself to his full five feet, because he stood at a particular angle to the audience, and because his timing was just right, the spectators answered with quivering guffaws.

Sometimes Jimmy sat on the stage, facing the audience in one of his most famous roles, that of Biddy Mulligan, the Pride of the Coombe. He sat with his wig and high-heeled shoes and nylons and a skirt, and perhaps an apron over the skirt, and he talked to the audience. As he talked, his skirt slipped up higher and higher until he would become suddenly conscious of the fact that his pink bloomers were showing. Or he was the duchess or the famous cinema actress, walking across the stage with a resplendent leg turned toward the audience, with his hair piled high, his lipstick and his earrings, and his bosom of exemplary proportions. He could be highly sentimental, as he was the night he impersonated Sir Harry Lauder, wearing the tartan and the *sporran* and the kilt, singing the old songs that had made Sir Harry famous, and bringing home to us that the world was somewhat poorer because the Scottish entertainer, the old man of the music halls, had recently died. Or he would sit on a chair in a seedy pub, portraying the man who had had a few pints too many and who was having trouble coordinating his limbs to keep upright, and a simple, innocuous situation was transformed into a moment of high comedy with richly tragic undertones.

When the show was over and one headed down the carpeted stairs of the Gaiety and out through the lobby and into the life and bustle of the city, it was sometimes hard to remember any coherent plot in any of the sketches Jimmy had performed. But it all seemed quite unimportant, for, when it was all over, what remained most clearly was the memory of having been for a few hours in the company of a marvelous little man who punned and quipped and clowned and whose humor was not, as it so often is in others, the outer edge of malice.

26

The Theater

It was my good fortune as a boy that these visits to the pantomime at Christmas formed only part of a much wider pattern of theater-going. For my father was deeply interested in the theater. He himself acted in plays, and, even when I was a child, he sometimes brought me with him to the Abbey for a dress rehearsal or to watch the setting up of a scene and the work of getting an act or even a full play ready. My earliest recollection of going to the theater is of a night when I was six or seven years old. A play was being performed at the Abbey, and my father had a part in it, and I was allowed to come along on the opening night. It was in the old Abbey Theater, which was later to be destroyed by fire and replaced by the present edifice. And this visit to the old Abbey was to be the first of very many.

Throughout my childhood and in my school days, whenever a worthwhile play was being performed in one of the many theaters in Dublin, I was nearly always brought along. There was much to choose from. There were four theaters in the middle of Dublin, and there were also a host of smaller halls and auditoriums where shows were put on from time to time. In the late 1940's and the early 1950's, there were several theater companies operating in the city, and, during most of the year, several new productions ran simultaneously, so that the avid theater-goer had a wide choice. During this time, the Abbey was a pale replica of its former glory. Apart from regular performances of O'Casey plays, which Dubliners always lined up to see, there was, for the most part, a dreary procession of plays that were known around Dublin as "kitchen comedies," plays usually with a rural setting and with characters and plots that were fair game for satire in the pantomimes or the other variety shows that could be seen during the year. The ghost of Barry Fitzgerald seemed to haunt the wings, and the plays I saw there frequently proved little more than an education in the life and characteristics of the stage Irishman, a creature beloved among the English and American tourists who came to the Abbey during the summer but, for the rest of us, a source of fascinated embarrassment. Fortunately, it was only a passing phase, but the passage seemed to many Dubliners unduly long.

In the other theaters, there was varied and often highly exciting fare. There were several companies, and each would lease a theater for a season. Visiting groups would come as well, such as Donald Wolfit and his company, from England, who put on seasons of Shakespeare, and Jean Vilar and the Théâtre National Populaire, from Paris. But, among the local groups, my favorite was that run by Hilton Edwards and Michael MacLiammoir, and, over many years,

I had the luck to be brought along to see the plays they performed. The keen excitement I still feel whenever I go to the theater is due in large measure to the marvelous world they opened up. Edwards tended to specialize in directing, but MacLiammoir was regularly on stage—a tall man with bulky shoulders, black hair, and brilliant eyes, who seemed to possess an unlimited fund of talent. Not only was he a first-class actor, but he could paint, and he frequently designed the sets for the plays they performed. He was also a writer, a good talker, and a character in his own right—a familiar sight around Dublin, heavily made up and with a great inclination to turn the simplest encounter into a theatrical one. He had one or two predictable mannerisms, such as a tendency to feel an earlobe as he delivered an amusing line, but, apart from that, he was a singular man. To all the parts he played, he brought an astonishing creativity, whether as the mad King Henry the Fourth in Pirandello's play of that name or as the evil Prince Bunin in *Anastasia.*

His brother-in-law Anew MacMaster had his own company and, during the war years, toured Ireland indefatigably, bringing the best of theater to small and often remote village halls. I saw him only a few times; the last occasion was at the Gaiety Theatre, where he played the role of Fagin in a stage version of *Oliver Twist.* He danced around the stage, a figure of cunning, brutishness, and animal fear. He lived near our house, and, once or twice, I saw him walking on the strand. One morning he swept into our grocery store, and the day seemed somehow brighter because of the manner in which he had set about buying a loaf of bread, resplendent in a bathrobe, his superb profile darkening shelves of corn flakes and mayonnaise and soup.

Such men brought luster to Dublin, and the chance to see them at work and at their finer moments was something I deeply valued.

27

On the Road

On the nights when I first went to the theater with my father and my mother, we used to have to go in on the bus; afterward we would come out and stand in line, often shivering after the warmth of the theater, waiting for another bus to take us home. But our lives were transformed completely when my father bought his first car, a Ford 8 of prewar vintage, which had belonged to a farmer somewhere north of Dublin who evidently had driven it only to Mass on Sundays: The car was in excellent condition when my father brought it home. That night, we were all gathered to admire it and to wait for the chance to have our first ride. From then on, we were to move around Ireland, for my mother and father were tireless travelers. During the war years, they had gone through the Wicklow Mountains and neighboring places on their bicycles. When my brother Ciaran and I were old enough to come along, my father put a small saddle on the crossbar of his bicycle where I could sit, while my brother sat on a device hanging off the handlebar at the front of my mother's bicycle. We would cycle fifteen or twenty miles into Wicklow, and we would have a picnic and would play until it was time to go home. With the car, our horizon broadened immeasurably. Every dry Sunday, we would take off on an expedition somewhere, and, during the summer, we would travel to the west, to the southwest, to the north, indeed, to every section of the country.

My father did all the driving, and, on a fine afternoon, as we headed somewhere, if he found himself getting tired, he would pull over to the side of the road, inform us that we would all be on our way shortly, slump unconscious over the wheel, and wake up five minutes later completely refreshed. Then we would resume our journey.

The first car, which we called Bessie, was succeeded by others, one of which we parked in the late evening outside Jervis Street Hospital, where we had gone to visit a patient. When we came out, it was gone. It had been stolen. We made our way sadly home by bus. My father called the police and, telling them what had happened, gave them the number of the car, and they assured him that they would see what they could do. On the following morning, my father went around to all the classes in his school in Marlborough Street and to all the classes in the school right behind his. He gave a description of the car, told them its number, and offered a reward to any schoolboy who could bring him information about it. That afternoon, when school was out, a dragnet spread through the entire city—

the Marlborough Street Irregulars, searching for the missing car. When classes were called to order the next day, a boy presented himself to my father and told him that he had found it. It was parked in a back street in a neighborhood of such respectability that the police rarely bothered to patrol it. My father brought the boy across to the local police station where he had reported the car missing and informed the police that it had been found. They seemed a little bit peeved that their work had been done for them with such speed and efficiency. When we got the car back, no damage had been done; all that were missing were a pair of gloves and a flashlight.

Sometimes, the car would give us trouble and my father would send word to Jimmy, an old friend of his, to come and help. We eagerly awaited his arrival, for not only was Jimmy a superb mechanic, but he was also a man whose talk brought us endless pleasure. He would come with his tool kit and his grizzled hair and a developing paunch, and he would open up the front of the car and stick his head in and examine what was going on. While he examined and turned knobs and fiddled with wires, he would talk, and the talk would lead to a reminder of some episode present or past, some adventure that, in the telling, was transformed into a drama in which he was a central comic figure.

"Frank and I were after being drinking. We were working late on the Christmas pressure. We used to get three weeks' pay for a four-day period. We went into a restaurant there in O'Connell Street, and the lady came up. Frank was readin' the menu, and it might as well have been a racin' docket. So I said, 'Oxtail soup, and chicken for two, a portion of chicken for two.'

" 'A *portion* of chicken?' she said.

" 'Miss, see them things. One, two. Two o' them.'

"She looked at us. I went over to the counter and got

the chickens. Lovely they were, too. Brought them over. We got our oxtail soup to give us an appetizer, and then we got stuck into the chicken. We made small work o' that. We come out o' there; I shook hands with Frank (his usual thing was to kiss you on the side o' the face); and then, 'God bless! God bless!' You'd see that for about five minutes. 'God bless!' He might be halfway up the street. 'GOD BLESS!' I went to stand at the bus stop.

" 'Mister, are ya waitin' on a bus?'

" 'Yes,' says I.

" 'Ah, they're gone off since half nine,' says he. The war was on at the time, you know. It was 1943. 'But there'll be one goin' up to the garage, up Connyngham Road.'

" 'Fair enough,' says I. When it came, I got on it, and I should o' gone inside. Instead, I stood on the platform with me hands in me pockets. The bus was goin' along. It was *flyin'*. And there's a hump where the path narrows to about twelve inches from the Liffey wall. The bus went vroomin' up the hump, and I went flyin' out and cracked me jaw on the Liffey wall. Next mornin', I was nearly able to put me food in without openin' me mouth. Me teeth was smashed an' all. Me mouth was big as a manhole. And I had to get the rest of the teeth out in a hurry up in Baggot Street. Then I had to get a palate with two teeth in it, and he told me to take my time now, eat sweets with 'em, and get used to 'em. Sure, I went into a pub for a couple o' drinks, and I was eatin' sweets, and I eat me teeth an' all. I was near destroyed.

"I had to go back after and get the rest out, and get a full plate with teeth on it. You don't get the same taste off your food at all. It has to go into your mouth; it has to take a trip back of the palate to let you taste it; and, when it's too hot after getting to the back of the palate, you have to open your mouth and drop your teeth. Ah, I've no time for that

game. Weddin's and funerals, that's all I use them for. At
the graveside, when the priest says, '*Requiescat in pace*,'
ah, you like to have your teeth in to say, 'Amen.' "

Our laughter pleases him. He takes off his spectacles, an
old pair that once belonged to my father, and he puts them
in his pocket. The action reminds him of visits to Wool-
worth's Stores in Henry Street, where there was a section
(outlawed in recent years) where spectacles could be
bought for a price far below that extracted by oculists or
opticians in any part of the city. On the display counter
were hundreds of pairs of glasses, and, if one had the req-
uisite nerve and patience, it was possible to find a suitable
pair. It meant standing for a long time, picking up one pair
after another, and trying them on.

This is what Jimmy used to do. On one occasion, he
bought a pair that he believed suited him. "I come out onto
Henry Street, and, there, at the top of the road, I seen this
fella I used to know at work. Because he was far away, I
raised me arm up over me head and waved so he could see
me. Sure, I crashed right into him. Oh, Mother of God, I
had to hurry back in and get another pair!"

Sometimes, having found a pair that satisfied the require-
ments of his vision, he would discover that the arms of the
spectacles reached an inch, perhaps two inches, behind his
ears. "All you had to do then was find one of the girls who
was havin' her cup o' tea: 'Excuse me, Miss,' and you'd dip
the arms in for a minute into the cup o' tea, to soften them,
don't you know, and bend 'em around to suit your ears."

Jimmy was born "in the year of the lamps," 1910, the
year the municipal authorities decided to erect new lampposts around the city. A commission was given to a firm
on the north side of Dublin, and, while the work was in
progress, two workmen fell into a vat of molten metal.
"They found a couple o' bits of cinders, and they put 'em

in a coffin and gave 'em a funeral up to Glasnevin Cemetery. That's why I can't stand it every time I see a dog using one of the lampposts. Sure, all I can do is say a prayer for the peace of their souls, God help them."

And he would straighten up and smile with satisfaction.

"There, now, the trouble's fixed. That carburetor wants watchin.' " He would linger; there would be a few more stories; and then he would go home.

It was Jimmy who taught me how to drive, and one afternoon we went up to Phoenix Park for that purpose. There were the trees and deer and a network of roads on which were other learners like myself, sitting grim-faced with concentration behind their wheels. Behind us were the spires and the rooftops of Dublin. Over to one side, the outline of the Dublin mountains. Driving around the park, I shifted into reverse, jammed on the brakes, tried out the clutch, and learned how I was supposed to behave in a crisis and what to do when I got caught in a narrow street. "*You* stop, son. Let *him* hit *you*, and then he'll have to pay the damages."

At the end of a long session of this, Jimmy said, "Let's drive into town." And I set off from Phoenix Park and drove down past Kingsbridge, past Guinness's and the barges, past the Four Courts, and beside me was the Liffey and ahead of me the bridges—the Ha'penny Bridge, O'Connell Bridge, and, beyond it, Butt Bridge and the cupola of the Customs House. The traffic got heavier, and I found myself with cars on every side. Jimmy, sitting beside me, said, "Ye're all right; carry on; change; that's a bit slow there; third to top there now." We passed the old antique stores and headed on until we came to O'Connell Bridge. We crossed that, too, and came out toward Sandymount and home. When we reached the tower at the end of our road, Jimmy said, "Watch that car in front of you," and

I did, and then I turned right into our road and came down as far as our house.

"Pull over there now, son," said Jimmy, and I did. And then he looked at me and smiled. "Ye're a great boy," he said, and, by the way he said it, I knew that what he meant was that I was no longer a boy.

I suppose he was right.